A Ferry Tale

Crossing the Delaware on the Cape May-Lewes Ferry

by William J. Miller, Jr.

Executive Director,
The Delaware River and Bay Authority

Published by
Gauge Corporation
Wilmington, Delaware 19801

*To my wife Ginny
and our family*

Project Coordinator: Ed Golin
Designer: Paul A. Miles
Photographs: Delaware River and Bay Authority
Cover Painting by Franklin Woodruff, Jr.

Third Edition, 1989-Revised

Printed in the United States of America
Library of Congress Card Number: 83-073487

ISBN:
Hard Cover: 0-911293-04-3
Soft Cover: 0-911293-03-5

Miller, William J. Jr.
A Ferry Tale:
Crossing the Delaware on the Cape May-Lewes Ferry

Also by William J. Miller, Jr.

Crossing the Delaware
The Story of the Delaware Memorial Bridge
The Longest Twin Suspension Bridge in the World

CONTENTS

Introduction 12

1. **How To Start A Ferry** 15
   ☐ Eureka! A Solution???

2. **Ferry Related Events** 25
   ☐ The Delaware Memorial Bridge
   ☐ The Chesapeake Bay Bridge-Tunnel

3. **Planning** 30

4. **The Layout** 34
   ☐ The Vessels
   ☐ The Terminals
   ☐ The Routing
   ☐ Berths and Bridges, Tanks and Tolls
   ☐ The Approach Roads
   ☐ Dredging

5. **Bits And Pieces** 45
   ☐ Studies
   ☐ Engineering Report
   ☐ Ferry Details
   ☐ Other Projects
   ☐ Schedules and Tolls
   ☐ Traffic and Revenue
   ☐ Other Income

6. **Packaging The Project** 56
   ☐ Financing
   ☐ Construction — What, How, Why?
   ☐ Dedication Ceremonies

7. **The Early Years** 66
   ☐ Other Details
   ☐ Five Years of Ferry Operations

8. **The Big Decision** 76
   ☐ Another Big Step

9. **Three New Vessels** 79

10. **The Turn Around** 86
    ☐ Black Budget
    ☐ A Minor Setback
    ☐ Capacity Problems

11. **MV New Del** 91

12. **Next?** 96

Appendices 106

ANECDOTES

Cape May 17
Lewes 19
Riding on The Ferry 20
In A Party Mood 21
The Cemetery 23
The Compact 26
Delaware Bay Bridges — Any More? 27
Marine Terms... 28
Radar 31
Coast Guard Station 32
Buying Old Ferry Vessels 35
Bad Advice 36
Crow Shoal 37
Ice in the Delaware Bay 44
Loran C 46
A Tale of Two Ferry Boats 51
Where Do They Come From?....................................... 52
Ferry Trailblazers... 54
What Happens to the Money? 55
Manning A Ferry 57
The Boomerang 58
Thumbs Up... 64
Red Rover, Red Rover, We Did Come Over 67
What, No Ice?... 68
A Long Ferry Ride 69
The First Ferry Accident—First Time Out of the Slip 70
The Lewes Approach Road 72
Looking Back 73
The TV Show 74
Hot Dogs & Beer 75
Out of Fuel... 77
Saved Poodle, Sunk Rabbit 78
Ferry Insurance... 84
Crossing Graph 86
Days Operational Graph 87
Where Does The Bay Start/Stop? 89
Twin Screw vs. Double Enders 93
Authority Police 98
Numbers and Dollars.. 101
For the Record 103
Up to Date 105

Acknowledgements

It is not intended for this narrative to be historical in relating the many events which have occurred over the years in the vicinity of Cape May and Lewes. In simple terms, the evolution of the Cape May-Lewes Ferry as it currently exists is outlined. From 1964 to the present is a relatively short time span. Nevertheless, the ferry project has accumulated many varied interests and they are herein outlined for those who are interested in this regard. It would be difficult to adequately express my thanks and appreciation to everyone who assisted in this assignment. Nevertheless, the interest, encouragement and assistance from the commissioners of the Delaware River and Bay Authority from New Jersey and Delaware, the staff assistance, particularly from Nolan C. Chandler, Theodore C. Bright and David S. Chapman, all of whom have served as General Manager of the ferry, my secretary, Eleanor Stradley and Rita Migliocco who preceded her and the typing assistance of Candy Drummond, are most appreciated. I would also like to acknowledge the guidance and advice of Ed Golin, president of Gauge Corporation; the editing and technical assistance of Kathy K. Demarest, editor for Delapeake Publishing Co.; and the graphic and layout suggestions of Paul A. Miles, designer for Delapeake Publishing Co.

William J. Miller, Jr.

Note:

While this narrative tells about the Cape May-Lewes Ferry system, history also tells us that other efforts to cross the Delaware Bay have been attempted over the years.

In 1898 for example, after a private company erected a pier in Cape May and after storm damage, the Queen Ann's Railroad started the Cape May-Lewes run in 1902. Extremely cold weather in 1903 and 1904 blocked bay traffic and after a ruinous fire in Baltimore in 1904, the firm went into receivership. When the line was acquired by the Maryland, Delaware and Virginia Railroad in 1905, the Cape May steamer route was immediately discontinued.

Source: "Roads Along The Chesapeake", John Hayman, 1979.

PREFACE

*(As reprinted from the program of the Cape May-Lewes Ferry
Dedication Ceremonies, June 30, 1964.)*

A ferry service does not begin in the drafting room of engineers nor in the swank offices of financiers. It begins, rather, in the imagination of men who want to get from one land base to another, across a body of water, in as straight a line as possible—and as quickly as possible.

This is how the Cape May-Lewes ferry began—back in the dawn of the histories of Delaware and New Jersey. From earliest days of colonization, men figured that the Delaware Bay and Atlantic Ocean could either be a barrier between the two states or a common bond.

The opening of the Cape May-Lewes ferry today caps the climax of dreaming, thinking and planning on how to "bridge" the barrier and establish what a New Jersey governor recently called "the betrothal of our two states."

Even before the coming of the Dutch, Swedish and English explorers in our area, the Indians ferried themselves across from one cape to another in their flimsy canoes. They didn't have to depend upon traffic studies to convince them of the importance of getting from one shore to the other.

The European settlers who followed them did likewise, although their craft was a lot more safe and dependable.

In the days before the Civil War, steamers would come down from Philadelphia, touch at Delaware ports, such as New Castle and Wilmington, and then proceed towards Cape May for weekend jaunts and summer holidays.

In the latter part of the 19th Century and early 20th Century, railroads and steamship companies combined their efforts to transport pleasure seekers across the Delaware Capes. That service died, but the dream of linking the two states with a ferry line did not fade. Men of southern Delaware and southern New Jersey stood on the shores of their respective states and in their minds' eyes could see a ferry service that would be beneficial to the entire area.

The only questions were—and they were major questions: How and who would start such a service?

Studies were made in the middle 1950's with great hopes that refused to be squelched by cynics and pessimists. Then came the big break which, oddly enough, grew out of a dispute between Delaware and New Jersey over the future of the Delaware Memorial Bridge.

In 1955, Gov. J. Caleb Boggs of Delaware and Gov. Robert B. Meyner of New Jersey began "conversations" about the mutual problems of their respective states. As they discussed the future of the Delaware Memorial Bridge, they also began to talk about "the ferry."

In the meantime, business and civic leaders of southern Delaware and southern New Jersey actively promoted the idea of a Cape May-Lewes ferry. They kept alive the plan which often faced defeat. It frustrated them that they were so close—and yet so far away with the absence of an agency that could bring them together.

Eventually, through intelligent understanding and a willingness to be partners in crossings of the Delaware River and Bay, the two states worked out a compact agreeable to the legislatures and the governors.

So was born the ten member Delaware River and Bay Authority, with blessings of the two states and the Congress. It had a directive to build other bridges across the Delaware and also establish a ferry between Cape May and Lewes.

Despite opposition in some quarters, the governors of the two states—Elbert N. Carvel of Delaware and Richard J. Hughes of New Jersey—worked together in harmony along with the authority representatives of their states.

From the time the authority was activated in February of 1963, its members proceeded with dispatch to establish the Cape May-Lewes ferry. It was visualized as "the missing link" in a route between New England and Florida and a stimulus in travel between central and southern Delmarva Peninsula and southern New Jersey.

Four ferries of the Kiptopeke-Cape Charles, Virginia line were purchased for $3,300,000. The vessels were refurbished and renamed in keeping with the Delaware-New Jersey "betrothal."

And so after many years of dreaming and planning the 16 mile expanse of water between Lewes and Cape May is spanned. The Delaware Bay is no longer a barrier, it is now a bond between two states.

By William P. Frank

To the Reader:

Perhaps my interest in the Cape May-Lewes Ferry system was stimulated after Elise and I happily accepted the invitation from Bill Miller and the Commissioners of the Delaware River and Bay Authority to participate in the dedication of the M.V. New Del, the newest of the four vessel fleet of the Cape May-Lewes Ferry system in July, 1981.

This book, which traces the ferry system since the 1950's, skillfully portrays the many elements which make up the system: the legislative requirements, the engineering and construction, the dredging, the vessel acquisition and operation, the financial constraints and perhaps most interesting, the many anecdotes which deal with interesting events over the years.

As you read the book, you'll realize that this transportation link across the lower Delaware Bay has had a tremendous impact in the economic development of lower Delaware and southern New Jersey. The continued growth in the ferry usage, as the traffic and earning statistics indicate, makes one wonder when the construction of a bridge might be necessary.

The interest and energy expended by Bill Miller in relating the saga of this "ferry tale" should be appreciated by each reader. I, indeed, commend him for his fine work.

Pierre S. du Pont
Governor
State of Delaware

To the Reader:

Eleven years ago, as the representative of former Governor William T. Cahill of New Jersey, I joined with Governor Russel W. Peterson of Delaware and with William J. Miller, Jr., Executive Director of the Delaware River and Bay Authority, to witness the signing of the contract documents for the construction of a new three vessel ferry fleet for the Cape May-Lewes Ferry system.

As an Assemblyman from North Jersey, I was very pleased to visit Cape May and to participate in the activities at that time. Today, I find the changes in events at the ferry are even more encouraging.

Vehicle and passenger usage at this most southerly transportation link in New Jersey has nearly doubled from my 1972 visit. A large part of the increased ferry usage is related to the interest in the Atlantic City casino activity which continues to surge in growth.

As Bill Miller indicates, there is every reason to believe that we can look forward to more crossings of the lower Delaware by more ferry vessels in the next few years, and then, as Governor du Pont questions, "When will we need a bridge?"

To memorialize this important transportation link is a worthwhile effort. I congratulate Mr. Miller for this fine achievement.

Thomas H. Kean
Governor
State of New Jersey

Introduction

The shrill whistle of the ferry vessel as it prepares to leave the terminal each day for its trip across the Delaware Bay quickens the pulse of adults and sends youngsters scurrying to their parents. Another ferry ride between Delaware and New Jersey is about to begin.

The Delaware Bay, as it approaches the Atlantic Ocean, can be a formidable foe or a lovely expanse of waterway dotted with the sails of summertime vacationers.

Oftentimes tankers waiting to be called inland to service oil refineries upstream sit silhouetted in the middle of the Bay. If one had the opportunity to talk to the pilots who traverse the river and bay waters, the exciting, variable conditions which exist would be particularly interesting.

In the winter, the ice conditions, at times, are so severe that ferry traffic must be stopped for safety purposes. In the summer, the vacation-minded, resort-oriented travelers are headed for the sun-filled beach areas.

There are those who use the ferry route as part of an "Ocean Hiway" routing from New England to Florida, seldom out of sight of the Atlantic Ocean. The recent Atlantic City gambling activities have generated another interest, and the ferry crossing provides

Like two ships passing in the night... two ferry boats, one headed for Cape May, the other for Lewes, glide by each other in the Delaware Bay.

access to that locale from lower Delaware, lower Maryland and parts of Virginia and beyond.

Since the inception of the ferry service in July 1964, thousands of crossings have occurred in fair weather and foul. This story relates to the individuals, the agencies and to all who enabled the ferry crossing service to begin and to continue its daily task of crossing the Bay.

*　*　*　*　*

On July 1, 1989 the ferry service completed 25 years of service. During the 1960's, the operation of the ferry system was difficult. The older vessels which had been acquired from Virginia were not suited to operate efficiently across the Delaware Bay. Traffic usage was slow in developing and revenues lagged far behind the ferry expenses. The most noticeable and favorable turn of events occurred when the Authority decided to sell the older vessels and replace them with new ones in the early 1970's.

Not only is the ferry service a noticeable tourist attraction for the lower Delaware Bay area, but it also provides a year round viable transportation route for many thousands of people.

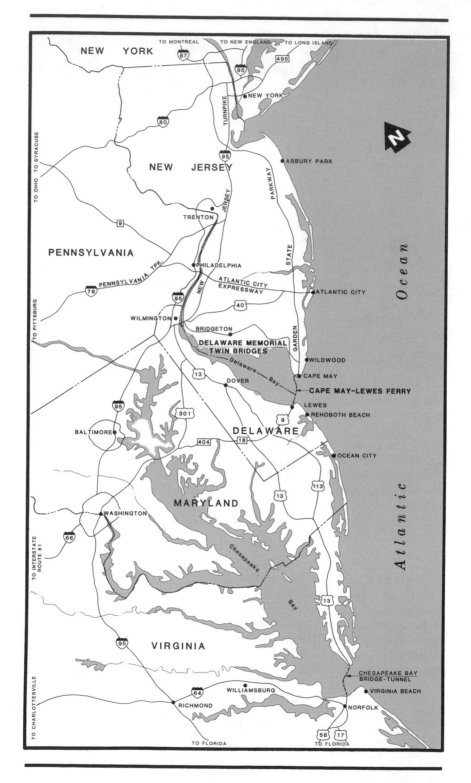

CHAPTER 1

HOW TO START A FERRY

One only needs to look at a map of the East Coast to see the relative position of southern New Jersey and lower Delaware to each other and then to quickly realize that southern New Jersey was, in fact, a dead end.

There was no way to span the 17 mile distance from Cape May to Delaware, nor did a solution to the problem seem to be reasonably available.

In the late 1940's and early 1950's, two major highways had been completed in New Jersey which carried traffic to and from the metropolitan New York area to southern New Jersey points. The famed New Jersey Turnpike was completed in 1951 and connected the New York area with the Delaware Memorial Bridge, which was also completed and opened to traffic in 1951, just a few months ahead of the turnpike.

On the east side of the state, paralleling the Atlantic Ocean shore line, the Garden State Parkway was completed. This new modern highway sped motorists to and from the resorts all the way to the southern terminus at Cape May ..... and then there was a dead end...

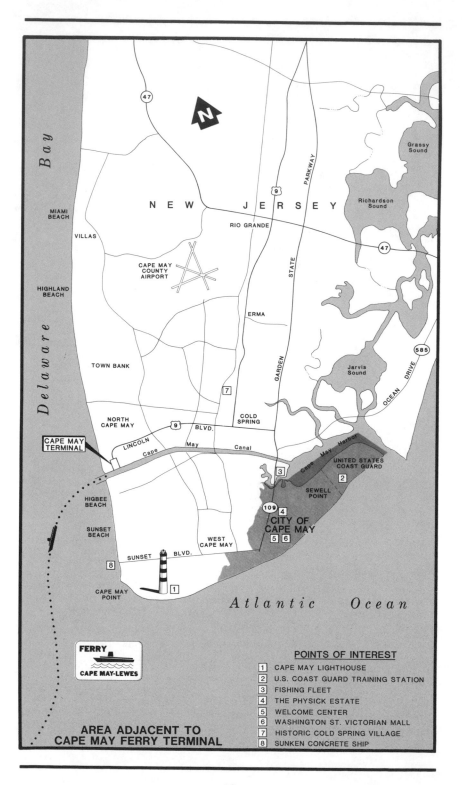

POINTS OF INTEREST

1. CAPE MAY LIGHTHOUSE
2. U.S. COAST GUARD TRAINING STATION
3. FISHING FLEET
4. THE PHYSICK ESTATE
5. WELCOME CENTER
6. WASHINGTON ST. VICTORIAN MALL
7. HISTORIC COLD SPRING VILLAGE
8. SUNKEN CONCRETE SHIP

AREA ADJACENT TO CAPE MAY FERRY TERMINAL

Cape May

Cape May County is the southernmost county in New Jersey, and Cape May City is the southernmost city in the state. Once known as Cape Island, the name is derived from a voyage to Delaware Bay in 1621 by Captain Cornelius J. Mey. The spelling of his name was later changed to May.

Cape May flourished as a popular summer resort in the late 1800's. The competition between it and other Atlantic Ocean resorts has increased over the years. Yet, Cape May has remained a favorite family resort which has retained its old time charm. The entire community has been designated a national historic landmark, no doubt due in part to the gingerbread Victorian homes and inns which line the seaside streets.

Cape May is at the southern end of the Garden State Parkway, some 150 miles south of New York City. It is 120 miles east of Washington, D.C. via the Cape May-Lewes Ferry and the Chesapeake Bay Bridge at Annapolis; 80 miles from Philadelphia and only one hour from Atlantic City.

Points of interest in Cape May include:
- The Lighthouse at Cape May Point
- The U.S. Coast Guard Training Center
- Fishing Fleet
- The Physick Estate, an 1881 Victorian Mansion
- Welcome Center
- Washington Street Victorian Mall
- Historic Cold Spring Village
- Sunken Concrete Ship

In 1953, however, an effort was made to solve the problem. At that time, the New Jersey legislature authorized the New Jersey Highway Authority to establish, construct, acquire, maintain, repair and operate a project to be known as the Cape May-Lewes Ferry.

There was not, however, any cooperative legislation enacted in Delaware.

In 1955, it was reported that the Hudson River Day Line, Inc. entered into an agreement with the New Jersey Highway Authority, the operators of the Garden State Parkway, providing for a ferry service between Cape May and Lewes. The developers were to provide plans for a speedy, convenient, safe and economical service across the Delaware Bay. The project faltered and was forgotten.

Even so, the New Jersey Highway Commissioner authorized a

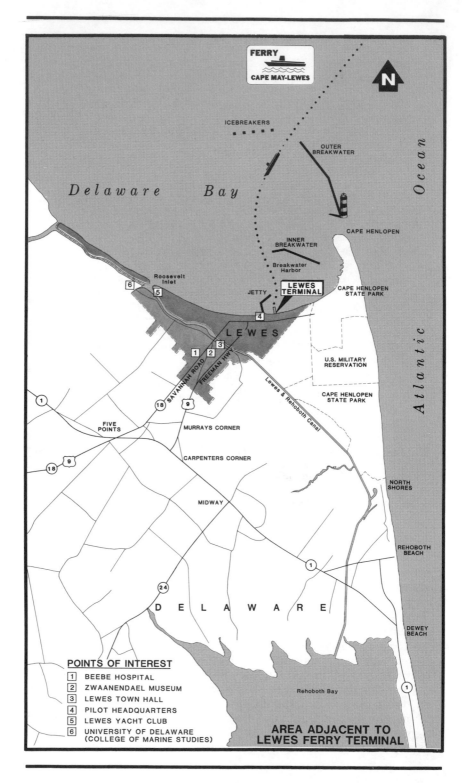

FERRY
CAPE MAY-LEWES

N

ICEBREAKERS

OUTER
BREAKWATER

Delaware *Bay*

Ocean

CAPE HENLOPEN

INNER
BREAKWATER

Breakwater
Harbor

Roosevelt
Inlet

⑥

⑤

CAPE HENLOPEN
STATE PARK

JETTY

LEWES
TERMINAL

④

L E W E S

U.S. MILITARY
RESERVATION

Atlantic

① ② ③

SAVANNAH ROAD

FREEMAN HWY

Lewes & Rehoboth Canal

CAPE HENLOPEN
STATE PARK

①

⑱ ⑨

FIVE
POINTS

MURRAYS CORNER

CARPENTERS CORNER

NORTH
SHORES

⑱ ⑨

MIDWAY

REHOBOTH
BEACH

①

②④

D E L A W A R E

DEWEY
BEACH

POINTS OF INTEREST

① BEEBE HOSPITAL
② ZWAANENDAEL MUSEUM
③ LEWES TOWN HALL
④ PILOT HEADQUARTERS
⑤ LEWES YACHT CLUB
⑥ UNIVERSITY OF DELAWARE
(COLLEGE OF MARINE STUDIES)

Rehoboth Bay

①

**AREA ADJACENT TO
LEWES FERRY TERMINAL**

report to survey the possibilities of a proposed ferry system across the lower Delaware Bay. The report contained a description of and recommendations for ferry terminals, ferry routes, connecting highways and proposed vessel designs together with an estimate of projected costs.

The report was dated July 15, 1956. In it were alternate locations for the ferry terminals and alternate routes for the crossing. On the New Jersey side, one terminal was studied for the Cape May Harbor via the Cape May Inlet. Another location was at the east end of the Cape May County Canal near the present ferry site.

In Delaware, consideration was given to a terminal facility at Roosevelt Inlet and another in the area of the Breakwater Harbor, in the vicinity of the present Lewes terminal.

Interestingly enough, this report, at that time, recommended the Roosevelt Inlet site primarily because of the added approach road and bridge requirements for the Breakwater Harbor location.

Lewes

With an altitude of 17 feet above sea level, Lewes (pronounced LOO-is) was first founded in 1631 by a group of settlers from Holland. Then called Zwaanendael, the agricultural and fishing village was soon destroyed by indians.

Located near Cape Henlopen (at one time called Cape Cornelius) the town has always been active in marine related events. It was bombarded by the British in the War of 1812 and the breakwaters, jettys and icebreakers scattered over the harbor area show evidence of the shipping interests.

The small town is the southernmost inland bay resort on the Delaware side of the Delaware Bay. It is located in Sussex County, the southernmost of the three Delaware counties, which at one time were a part of Pennsylvania. Today, Lewes retains the charm of the quaint atmosphere in which it is located.

Points of interest in Lewes include:
- *Beebe Hospital*
- *Zwaanendael Museum*
- *Lewes Town Hall*
- *Pilot Headquarters*
- *Lewes Yacht Club*
- *University of Delaware College of Marine Studies*

And, on the New Jersey side of the bay, the report recommended the Cape May Harbor site primarily because of shallow water over the shoals approaching the western end of the Cape May County Canal.

RIDING
ON THE FERRY

When the mercury denotes
    Sultry summer heat,
Then the spacious ferry-boats
    Afford a cool retreat,
On a shady upper deck,
    Joined by friends so merry,
Bless me! ain't it pleasant,
    Riding on the ferry?

Back and forth from shore to shore,
    On the rippling river,
Watching spray beads rise and fall,
    Where the sunbeams quiver;
Reveling in the cooling breeze,
    Every one is cherry;
Bless me! ain't it pleasant,
    Riding on the ferry?

Now you're sitting vis-a-vis
    With a charming creature,
Happiness is in her eye,
    Joy in every feature.
"Isn't this superb?" she asks,
    "Yes," you answer, "very."
Bless me! ain't it pleasant,
    Riding on the ferry?

Thus the heated hours are passed, —
    Laughing, joking, singing;
Joyous shouts from happy groups
    On the cool breeze ringing.
Now you see your charmer home,
    Feeling blithe and merry,
'Cause engaged to go tomorrow
    Riding on the ferry.

Source: George W. Osborne in American Ferry Boats,
    John Perry, 1957.

When the routes were more closely reviewed, the 21 - 25 nautical mile length between the Roosevelt Inlet - Cape May Harbor route contrasted with the 17 mile distance between the Inlet and the west canal location. The shorter trip was ultimately preferred.

The report proposed that two ferry vessels be used. Each would accommodate 115 - 120 vehicles and as many as 800 passengers. The ships would be 350 feet in length, have a beam of 71 feet and a loaded draft of 8 feet. The estimated cost, at that time, was $3 million each.

Terminal facilities, approach roads and dredging in the affected areas brought the total estimated construction cost to $12 million. The report suggested the two vessels leave Cape May and Lewes respectively at 6 a.m. and make 11 round trips daily. There were no provisions for maintenance work or drydocking. Presumably, fuel, maintenance and crew arrangements were to be provided separately in Delaware and New Jersey.

The report estimated that the ferry service would be inoperable about 10 days each year because of high wave conditions.

A review of the $12 million cost estimate is interesting. A 35 year bond issue at 3½ percent (a reasonable interest rate at that time) would require annual debt service payments for interest and amortization of $580,000. In addition, annual maintenance expenses were listed in the report to total $1.1 million.

The report did not include cost for maintenance dredging, approach roads or concession buildings.

Even more surprising, the report gave no estimates of the

In a Party Mood

In the mid 1950's, Delaware Governor J. Caleb Boggs and members of the General Assembly were invited to a dinner party at Cape May by the New Jersey ferry advocates. After hours of conviviality, plenty of food and a general good time, the party broke up and the Delaware contingent returned, promising to favorably consider the ferry crossing idea.

The Governor later recalled that one of the prominent Delaware legislators returned with him in the Governor's limousine. As they travelled, late into the night, the legislator tapped the Governor and said, "You know, Governor, I don't think we should rush into this ferry legislation too quickly."

"What's the problem?" asked the Governor. "Oh, there is no problem, but I enjoy these parties so much, perhaps we can encourage them to have one or two more before we vote."

number of vehicles expected to use the ferry crossing, and therefore, there were no estimates of expected income. Toll rates were not discussed.

Nevertheless, the report was favorably received by southern New Jersey officials, particularly in Cape May County. The fact that there was little or no interest in southern Delaware did not deter those who supported the idea from vigorously pursuing it.

In the mid 1950's, an attempt was made to pass legislation in the Delaware General Assembly which would assist in the initiation of a ferry service. The 1956 report was to serve as a springboard to generate support for the project.

As one could expect, there was a divided reaction between the northern and southern Delaware legislators. The voting crossed party lines and despite the endorsement of the Republican governor and the Democratic state chairman, the measure did not pass the Assembly. The ferry crossing idea was again delayed.

Eureka! A Solution???

While advocates were being frustrated in their attempts to push for a ferry system, problems were developing at the northern end of the state of Delaware, particularly surrounding the continued operation of the Delaware Memorial Bridge.

Prior to the opening of the Delaware Memorial Bridge on August 16, 1951, the only means of crossing the Delaware River in the vicinity of Wilmington was on the New Castle-Pennsville Ferry. This ferry service, however, proved inadequate in meeting the constantly increasing traffic demands of the area at that time.

After many years of discussion, planning and legislative efforts, hampered also by the impact of World War II, legislation was finally approved in 1945 which authorized the Delaware State Highway Department to construct, operate and maintain a Delaware River crossing in the vicinity of Wilmington.

Subsequently, the New Jersey Legislature enacted legislation in 1946 permitting the project to go forward.

Also in 1946, Congress enacted legislation authorizing the construction, operation and maintenance of a bridge over the Delaware River. Pertinent conditions of this legislation provided that:

- Delaware be authorized to proceed with the project, subject to the approval of the location and design of the bridge by the War and Navy Departments.
- Tolls be assessed for the use of the bridge.
- Tolls be adjusted to provide funds for maintenance and operation and for amortization requirements of a bond issue, which would provide funds for the project. However, it also provided that the bridge should be paid for within 30 years and be operated toll free after it was paid for.

Cemetery Dedication—Mrs. Hazel Brittingham (left) of the Lewes Historical Society and Mrs. Robert Kennedy of the Col. David Hall Chapter of the Daughters of the American Revolution dedicate the monument marking the Unknown Sailors' Cemetery near the ferry terminal in Lewes.

The Cemetery

At the request of the Lewes Historical Society, a plaque has been erected in the Lewes Terminal area to mark the final resting place of the unknown seafaring men whose remains are reportedly located there.

For more than 150 years, unclaimed bodies of seamen washed ashore were buried in unmarked graves, many at or near the site of the ferry terminal. The inscription on the plaque reads as follows:

UNKNOWN SAILORS' CEMETERY

Lewes has been a Port-of-Call and a
Harbor-of-Refuge since the 17th century.
For generations during the age of sail, a
public burial ground in this immediate locality
became the final resting place for hundreds
of sailors who lost their lives and whose
unidentified bodies were here cast ashore.
In remembrance of those persons whose remains
are sheltered on this shore, this memorial is placed.
May they find eternal repose.
1983
Erected by the Delaware River and Bay Authority in cooperation with the Col. David Hall Chapter of the Daughters of the American Revolution and The Lewes Historical Society.

* * * * * * *

An 1867 atlas contains an enlargement of the Town of Lewes. On this drawing, a cemetery symbol is delineated in the vicinity of the Lewes Terminal area.

A $40 million issue of revenue bonds was sold in June 1948, and work started on the bridge. The bridge was opened to traffic August 16, 1951.

When the original Delaware legislation was adopted for the bridge, the New Castle-Pennsville Ferry carried about 1.3 million vehicles annually. It was estimated that 3.6 million vehicles would use the bridge in 1951. However, in 1952, the first full year the bridge was open, traffic volume soared and so did the revenue. Nearly 7 million vehicles crossed the bridge that year.

The accompanying traffic problems were not anticipated nor were any rapid solutions offered.

And to add to the problem, unanticipated revenue from the bridge accelerated the bond payment. By 1956, it looked as if the bonds would be paid off in the early 1960's, at which time tolls would cease and there would be no revenue for bridge maintenance or operations.

Delaware sought relief from Washington. The state wanted permission to continue tolls to build another crossing and approach roadways. New Jersey, however, opposed the plan and asked for an opportunity to negotiate an agreement with Delaware.

As a result, Governor J. Caleb Boggs of Delaware and Governor Robert B. Meyner of New Jersey appointed a Conferee Committee to negotiate an agreement.

At the first meeting in December 1958, Governor Boggs stated that some of the broader questions involved were:
- the need for another crossing to supplement the Delaware Memorial Bridge.
- the need for a Bay ferry.
- the need to continue toll charges on the Delaware Memorial Bridge.
- the feasibility or practicability of a bi-state agency to administer the operation of crossings.

Ultimately, the committee prepared draft legislation for the two states. Optimism for a ferry service across the lower Delaware Bay really began at this point.

CHAPTER 2

FERRY
RELATED EVENTS

The Conferees met well into 1959 working out the details of a compact between the State of Delaware and the State of New Jersey. Finally on November 1, 1959, a press release stated:

- The Conferees ... have completed their report and submitted it to each Governor and to the members of the Legislature in each state.
- The report recommends the adoption of a compact to create "The Delaware River and Bay Authority." Five commissioners are to represent each state, a majority of the commissioners from each state is required for any action, either Governor may veto any action, and the chairman and vice chairman shall alternate between the states.
- The initial project assigned the new agency is the operation of the Delaware Memorial Bridge. Immediate action to construct another crossing is to follow.
- The need for another bay crossing, probably by ferry, needs to be addressed.

The joint report, which was submitted by the Conferees, stated: "this agency should be the only bi-state authority of the States of Delaware and New Jersey which will serve as the conduit or medium through which the states may at all times act with respect to all matters of common interest to them."

The Delaware River and Bay Authority compact legislation was approved by the States of Delaware and New Jersey and the Congress of the United States in 1962.

The Compact

Between 1957 and 1959, a group of conferees representing New Jersey and Delaware met frequently to devise and recommend a plan to (a) jointly operate the Delaware Memorial Bridge, (b) construct a second bridge and additional crossings as needed, including a ferry system for the lower bay area and (c) plan, develop and operate related transportation facilities and projects between New Jersey and Delaware.

The agency, still in operation, consists of five members from each state. In New Jersey, one is required for Salem County, Cumberland County and Cape May County. The two other members are not designated.

In Delaware, two members come from New Castle County, two from Sussex County and one from Kent County.

In both states, not more than three of one political party may serve at any time. In each state, the terms are for five years, so that normally a member could be replaced or reappointed in each state each year. However, a member continues service until he is replaced by the Governor and confirmed by the respective State Senate.

A quorum consists of three members of each state and the affirmative vote of three members of each state is required for any action. Each Governor has veto power over any action.

The Commissioners elect their own Chariman and Vice Chairman, each holding office for a two-year term, then rotating to the alternate state.

Other powers and duties are covered in the compact legislation. One of the more unique provisions is that the Authority police have, regardless of their residence, all powers usually exercised by police in each state when involved in Authority facilities or projects.

The Authority is not funded by either state. It operates exclusively with the revenue collected at the toll facilities.

This action provided for the organization of the Authority on February 6, 1963. One of the first items of business, as shown in the minutes of the first meeting, (attended by both the Governor of Delaware and the Governor of New Jersey) was a proposal to update earlier feasibility reports concerning a Delaware Bay ferry between Lewes and Cape May.

The Cape May-Lewes Ferry project was again on its way.

The Delaware Memorial Bridge

There was then, and probably always will be, a very close relationship between the activities of the Delaware Memorial Bridge and other crossings of the lower Delaware River and Bay, particularly the Cape May-Lewes Ferry service.

The initiation of the bridge construction in 1948 was, in reality, the beginning of a new era in transportation, particularly for crossings of the Delaware River and Bay between the two states.

Just as there was a study prepared as far back as 1956 to investigate the feasibility of a ferry crossing between the two capes at the southern end of each state, there was in the early 1960's a study for a crossing of the Delaware River between Cumberland County, New Jersey and Kent County, Delaware.

This study was paid for jointly by the New Jersey Highway Department and by the Delaware Interstate Highway Division, then the operator of the Delaware Memorial Bridge.

After the creation of the bi-state Authority in 1963 all future crossing studies and related activities have been performed under the direction of the Delaware River and Bay Authority.

But, not only was the bridge the stimulus for the initiation of legislation creating the Authority, it also was intended to provide financial support for other crossing projects in the years to come, to the extent that they were in turn, able to be justified.

This really means that the bridge toll income could be used to support the ferry service and perhaps in the years to come, support other crossings of the Delaware between the two states.

Delaware Bay Bridges - Any More?

In 1963, or about the time the legislation creating the Delaware River and Bay Authority was enacted, the New Jersey Highway Department requested the Delaware Interstate Highway Division to join with them in a study of the feasibility of a river crossing between Cumberland County, New Jersey and Kent County, Delaware, in the vicinity of Bridgeton and Smyrna.

The results of the study were received after the creation of the new Authority and were delivered to the newly-appointed commissioners and to the New Jersey Highway Department.

The report stated that a suspension bridge could be built at this location, but that because of limited approach roads, the financial feasibility of the crossing could not be assured. An updated version of the report in 1970 stated that possibly by 1985 the feasibility could be expected to improve. The 1973 subsequent gas crisis in all probability delayed any serious consideration.

The Chesapeake Bay Bridge-Tunnel

Just as there has been a connection between the Delaware Memorial Bridge and the beginning of the Cape May-Lewes Ferry service, there also has been a connection between the ferry service and the construction of another bridge-tunnel crossing many miles away across the Chesapeake Bay connecting the Eastern Shore region of the Del-Mar-Va peninsula with Norfolk, Virginia.

In the early 1960's, Virginia decided to proceed with the immense project of building a 21-mile crossing across the lower Chesapeake Bay. The crossing ultimately required the building of two tunnels, two bridges, four man-made islands and 23 miles of roadway, including the approaches.

Marine Terms

Aboard the vessel, the traveler may wish to use and understand some commonly used terms.

CAPTAIN: The officer in charge of all vessel activities. The captain must be licensed by the U.S. Coast Guard.

CHIEF ENGINEER: This crew member is in charge of all engine room activities and equipment on the ship.

STARBOARD: Looking forward on the ship, the starboard side is to the right.

PORT: The reverse of starboard.

STERN: The back or rear of the vessel.

BOW THRUSTER: Special propellers installed in the forward part of the vessel hull for maneuvering assistance.

DRAFT: The distance between the waterline and the bottom of the vessel, usually measured in feet. (seven feet on the current ferry vessels)

BRIDGE: On a ship, this term refers to the area from which the captain operates the vessel. This area is also referred to as the pilot house or wheel house.

SCREWS, PROPS and WHEELS: Terms frequently used to denote the propellers on a vessel.

BUOYS: Markers to indicate the location of specific areas or conditions, such as shallow water or obstructions.

MV: Motor Vessel is used to designate vessels with propulsion equipment such as the diesel engines on the MV Delaware.

SS: Designates steam powered vessels, or 'steamship', as in the SS New Jersey.

LST: The MV Cape Henlopen was a converted Landing Ship Tank acquired from the U.S. Navy after World War II.

The world's largest bridge-tunnel project built at a cost of $200 million was opened to traffic in 1964 replacing a ferry service, which had served the same route for many, many years.

This, then, provided the relationship between the Chesapeake Bay Bridge-Tunnel and the Cape May-Lewes Ferry project: The Bridge-Tunnel opening date of April 15, 1964 made the fleet of ferry vessels owned by that agency available.

It was hardly a surprise, therefore, to see in the Authority minutes dated April 30, 1963 a reference to the availability of the ferry vessels from Virginia. The timing for the new ferry service across the Delaware Bay was beginning to develop.

CHAPTER 3

PLANNING

By early 1963, a ferry crossing between New Jersey and Delaware seemed more of a reality.

- The Governors of Delaware and New Jersey endorsed the project.
- The newly formed Delaware River and Bay Authority voted at its first organizational meeting to update a previous report on the ferry.
- The New Jersey Highway Commissioner agreed to allow the Authority to use his file on the ferry studies.

Work on the feasibility study was temporarily stalled in March of that year when the Highway Commissioner and the engineering firm could not agree on costs.

This impasse, however, was resolved, and by the April meeting, reports containing details of a proposed crossing were presented to the commissioners. The preliminary engineering report showed terminal locations, dredging requirements, traffic and revenue studies, proposed toll and ferry schedules, seasonal uses and the availability of the ferry vessels from the Chesapeake Bay and Tunnel District in early 1964.

A financing plan was also presented which combined the proposed Cape May-Lewes Ferry system with the second structure for the Delaware Memorial Bridge. The plan assumed:

- A Cape May-Lewes Ferry service would be established at the earliest practical date.
- The ferry vessels to be used would be purchased from the Chesapeake Bay and Tunnel District and be delivered in early 1964.
- The ferry terminal facilities and approach roads would be completed within one year.
- An urgent need for the second structure of the Delaware Memorial Bridge, which would require 3 to 4 years to construct.
- For financing purposes, the proposed ferry system and the new parallel bridge project would be combined.
- Based on estimates by consulting engineers for costs of construction, maintenance and operation and the estimates on traffic volumes and revenues by traffic engineers, financing the combined projects seemed feasible.

Ferry captain watches one of the two radar screens which are on each vessel.

Radar

Every ferry rider should know that there are two radar sets in use on each vessel. The spinning device above the pilot house is the antenna unit for the radar.

When necessary, the captain uses the radar to assist him in navigating the bay crossing, usually needed during bad weather, when visibility is reduced or obscured. Night time operations also are assisted by the radar equipment.

The radar units include a "screen" on which features which are delineated by the tracking action of the equipment are portrayed. In effect, the captain "sees" a map-like picture of the conditions which exist - they can be movable or stationary, another vessel, a jetty, the shore line or in some cases extreme wave conditions.

The licensing conditions for the crew of the vessel by the U.S. Coast Guard require that the captain be certified as proficient in the use of the radar units. Each one is another tool which is used to make the crossing a safe one for each passenger.

The old Coast Guard Station now serves as headquarters for the Pilots Association of the Bay and River Delaware, adjacent to the Lewes Terminal area.

Coast Guard Station

An old Coast Guard Station had been built adjacent to the ferry terminal location in Lewes. After many years of activity, the property was abandoned and eventually turned over to the University of Delaware to be used, perhaps, as an adjunct to the newly founded College of Marine Studies.

The Pilots Association of the Bay and River Delaware, looking for a headquarters in Lewes, was given title to the Coast Guard Station property and building by the University. In turn, the Pilots paid for a new university building at the Marine College, nearby.

Subsequently, the Pilots rebuilt the Coast Guard Station and now occupy it. The new building is immediately north of and adjacent to the Lewes Ferry Terminal. The launch area for the launches which transport the pilots to and from the tankers and other vessels moving up and down the river is also located next to the ferry slips.

The proposed financing plan outlined the need for interim capital for the purchase of ferry vessels, real estate and right of way purchases, terminals and approach roads and other related expenses.

With the adoption of the financing proposals, the steps to be taken to proceed with specific details concerning the ferry project could now be undertaken. The commissioners adopted the proposed financing plan and accordingly, a team of consulting engineers, traffic engineers, bond counsel and investment bankers was engaged to proceed with their respective assignments.

In addition, the Authority staff, on a day-by-day basis, coordinated, monitored, reviewed and processed the activities and procedures of the specialists.

The Authority's regular monthly minutes provide a condensed summary of activities, highlighting the progress of the separate assignments and to some degree, elaborating on the more important elements.

For many years, the dreams of a crossing were discussed by residents of Cape May County, New Jersey and Sussex County, Delaware. On a clear day it was frequently possible to look across the bay and see the shoreline on the opposite side. On a clear night and much more easily, one could see the reflection of the illuminated areas in the sky. Now, in the minds of many, the outlines of ferry boats were on the horizon.

Almost forgotten were the meetings in Trenton and in Dover when members of the legislature in each state were being buttonholed to vote for a ferry; in each case, the upstate contingent always denied the downstate group the opportunity they desired. But a way had been found to provide the ferry service and the project was indeed on its way to being accomplished. The Authority was concentrating on specific details on the ferry project.

CHAPTER 4

THE LAYOUT

The Vessels

As reported earlier, the construction of the 21-mile bridge and tunnel crossing of the Chesapeake Bay between Norfolk, Virginia and the southern end of the Del-Mar-Va Peninsula was scheduled for completion in the spring of 1964.

The Virginia agency was eager to sell the ferry vessels which had linked the two areas before the bridge construction.

The timely availability of the ferry vessels in Virginia encouraged Delaware Bay ferry advocates to press for the new crossing to coincide with the completion of the Chesapeake Bay Bridge-Tunnel.

With no other buyer in sight, Virginia ferry owners were anxiously pushing the Authority to agree to purchase their vessels.

In June of 1963, the commissioners formally authorized the financing and establishment of a Cape May-Lewes Ferry system and agreed to make a trip to Norfolk to inspect the ferries in operation.

At the July 1963, Authority meeting, an agreement was presented and approved which authorized the purchase of seven ferry vessels at a total cost of $4 million. The agreement further stipulated that the vessels, after delivery at Cape May, must be certified by the U.S. Coast Guard for use in the proposed route between Cape May and Lewes. Appropriate spare parts and other related equipment were included in the total cost.

Ultimately, the Authority only purchased four of the ferry vessels for $3.3 million, realizing that the new ferry service did not need the entire Virginia fleet. The vessels were:

- SS Pocahontas
- SS Princess Anne
- SS Del Mar Va
- MV Virginia Beach

Coincidental with the purchase, the Authority also agreed to offer jobs to the employees at the Virginia ferry location who wished to relocate to Delaware or New Jersey.

The Authority hired former manager of the Virginia ferry systems Nolan C. Chandler and several of his assistants to manage the new ferry. This move enabled the ferries to be handled by experienced personnel and also satisfied Coast Guard licensing requirements for vessels of this size and class.

Buying Old Ferry Vessels

The ferry vessels in use across the Chesapeake were varied in type, style and age. The SS Pocahontas, for instance, was built at the Pusey and Jones Shipyard in Wilmington in the 1930's. In later years, it was cut apart and lengthened by inserting an additional section in the middle of the ship.

The MV Virginia Beach was a converted LST naval vessel from World War II. The Virginia Beach had a diesel powered engine while the others had steam engines.

The Authority hired a naval architect to survey the vessels and recommend a fair price for them. The Virginia people did the same, and a final price was negotiated. One of the most important conditions concerning the ferry vessels was that they had to be certified by the U.S. Coast Guard for operation in the Delaware Bay area and that any costs involved in meeting this requirement were to be borne by the seller, the Virginia agency.

The renovations required by the Coast Guard were unexpectedly severe and cost the Virginia agency several hundred thousand dollars.

The Terminals

In July 1963, the Authority agreed with the consulting engineers' recommendation that the Lewes Ferry Terminal should be located adjacent to the Coast Guard Station. Planning for the necessary approach roads to this site was then started.

The engineers had also selected the location for the Cape May Terminal to be next to the Cape May Canal as it entered the Delaware Bay.

The two terminals were now located - but which was to be the headquarters for the ferry? The engineers said that the decision could be made by a flip of a coin, to the consternation of the commissioners!

Politics came into play. Since the Delaware Memorial Bridge headquarters was located in Delaware, the commissioners reasoned, it was judiciously logical that the ferry headquarters should be located in New Jersey. The Lewes Chamber of Commerce, trying to entice the headquarters to Lewes, offered some "free" land and other inducements, but the ferry terminal headquarters was targeted for Cape May.

Later events made this decision a far reaching one.

The location of the headquarters led to other important decisions. For example, a large storage tank was required for the steamship fuel. Also, a maintenance shop area would be required as well as facilities to store supplies and materials for the all important food and concession services to be offered aboard each ferry.

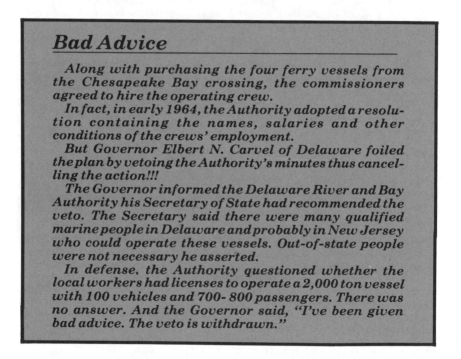

Bad Advice

Along with purchasing the four ferry vessels from the Chesapeake Bay crossing, the commissioners agreed to hire the operating crew.

In fact, in early 1964, the Authority adopted a resolution containing the names, salaries and other conditions of the crews' employment.

But Governor Elbert N. Carvel of Delaware foiled the plan by vetoing the Authority's minutes thus cancelling the action!!!

The Governor informed the Delaware River and Bay Authority his Secretary of State had recommended the veto. The Secretary said there were many qualified marine people in Delaware and probably in New Jersey who could operate these vessels. Out-of-state people were not necessary he asserted.

In defense, the Authority questioned whether the local workers had licenses to operate a 2,000 ton vessel with 100 vehicles and 700- 800 passengers. There was no answer. And the Governor said, "I've been given bad advice. The veto is withdrawn."

The Routing

Many routes between Lewes and Cape May were considered for the new ferry crossing - one almost needs a marine chart to grasp the differences in the choices.

While it may seem as if a pilot could just steer a ferry across the Delaware Bay by simply dodging man-made jetties and other river traffic, that is not the case.

What is seen above water doesn't reflect conditions on the bottom of the bay under the water. Water depth is an important factor in the ferry route.

In contrast to relatively deep water in the Chesapeake Bay, water depths across the Delaware Bay are quite varied and along the shore lines in each state, quite shallow.

However, the Authority had already decided to buy the Virginia ferry vessels. Now they had to worry about adequate water depths in which the vessels could operate safely.

The 1956 report tried to address and compare the alternate 21-mile "outside" route with the shorter 17-mile "inside" route. Storm conditions, trip lengths and related fuel costs as well as vessel draft conditions were compared. Obviously, the shorter route would be preferred. Not only would the crossing time be more attractive but the fuel savings, passenger comfort and speedier trip time would be advantageous. Yet, dredging would be required for this route, and the Authority wondered how much dredging would cost and how often it would be required.

Dredging became a commonly used word distinctly related to the ferry operation.

In the 1956 report, the routes (see map next page) either went outside of Cape May to Roosevelt Inlet or veered north of the Cape May Canal to the Inlet.

Crow Shoal

Travelling across the Delaware Bay one might assume it an easy task to navigate a ship or small boat in the bay waters.

Yet, looks are deceiving. Over the years many ship wrecks and groundings have occurred due to the shallow water, shoals, bars, reefs and the like. Contrary to the view one has from the deck of a ferry vessel, there are many shallow water areas to be traversed as one crosses the Bay. One of the most prominent is Crow Shoal, a relatively shallow water area the ferry crossed for many years. To do so, however, the area required constant dredging, costing millions. For many years, ferry captains had to search carefully for the four buoys marking the corners of the dredged area on every crossing, day and night, good weather and bad.

To their relief, the new shallow draft ferries enabled pilots to travel routes where dredging was not required. A big sigh of satisfaction and another event in the history book of ferry activities passed when these shallow draft ferries were built and placed into service in 1974.

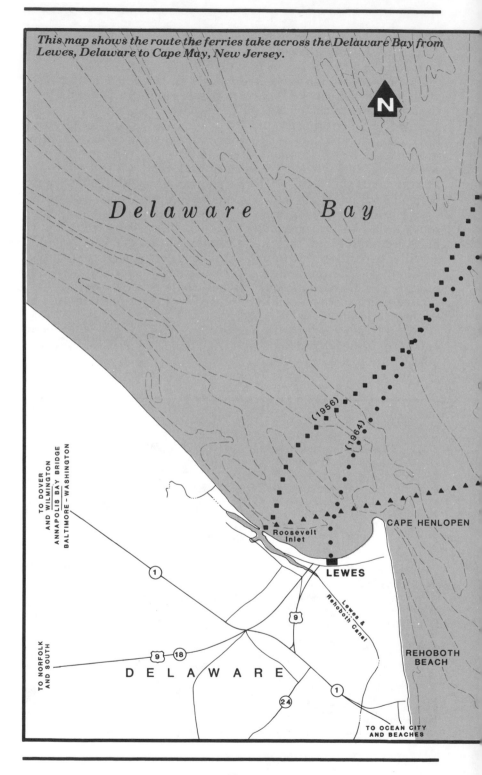

This map shows the route the ferries take across the Delaware Bay from Lewes, Delaware to Cape May, New Jersey.

N

Delaware Bay

(1956)

(1964)

Roosevelt Inlet

CAPE HENLOPEN

LEWES

Lewes & Rehoboth Canal

TO DOVER
AND WILMINGTON
ANNAPOLIS BAY BRIDGE
BALTIMORE – WASHINGTON

1

9

9 18

TO NORFOLK
AND SOUTH

D E L A W A R E

REHOBOTH
BEACH

1

24

TO OCEAN CITY
AND BEACHES

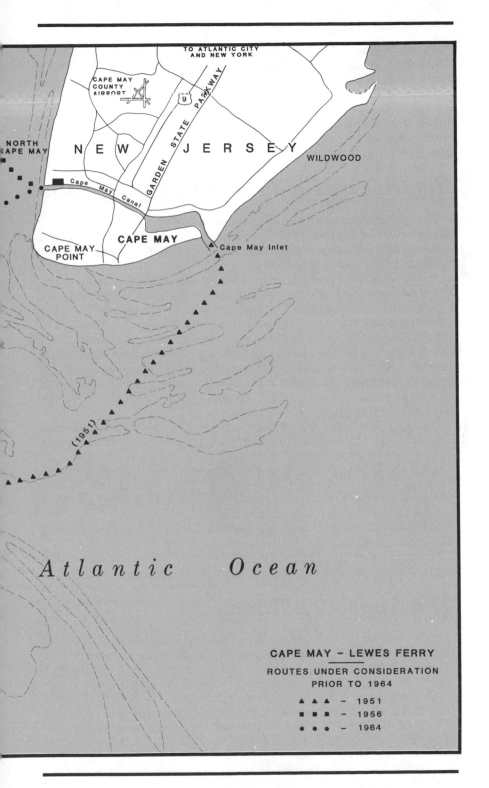

CAPE MAY – LEWES FERRY

ROUTES UNDER CONSIDERATION
PRIOR TO 1964

▲ ▲ ▲ – 1951
■ ■ ■ – 1956
● ● ● – 1964

In 1963, the final selection changed the route to the Lewes Harbor of Refuge area and to the Cape May Canal transversing Crow Shoal to shorten the route.

The selected route would require dredging in the Lewes Terminal area, in the Cape May Canal and across Crow Shoal, the latter being the most formidable and the most expensive to maintain. Some changes in the route occurred in the later years, but the basic crossing remains the same today.

Berths and Bridges, Tanks and Tolls

There was so much enthusiasm for the ferry project that many plans were underway months before the report containing the total project picture was completed and accepted by the Authority.

When the report was delivered:

- The Virginia ferry vessels had been purchased.
- The Cape May and Lewes Terminal locations were selected.

Since the headquarters for the ferry was to be at Cape May, the office building for the staff would need to be larger than the Lewes office. A maintenance shop was provided and a large fuel tank for the Bunker C fuel was required for the three steamships. The fourth vessel, a converted LST, used diesel fuel and needed a smaller, separate tank. The Bunker C fuel is relatively heavy and in winter requires heating and covered pipelines for the fuel to be pumped from the tank to the vessels.

Initially, the four vessels were expected to operate on a 24-hour schedule. Berths were required for each vessel for normal operations, and storage or maintenance. When the Authority purchased the ferry fleet, it also acquired transfer bridges for each location. The four bridges, two at Cape May and two at Lewes, permit the vehicles to drive on and off the vessels. They can adjust vertically for varying tide conditions.

Finally, both terminals would need parking areas for the waiting vehicles as well as toll collection facilities.

Lewes needed only a small reception building and no provision for fuel or water or other maintenance requirements.

The Approach Roads

In New Jersey, the ferry terminal is located adjacent to Lincoln Boulevard, a local township road. This road was extended by the Authority with a new 1.8 mile roadway to connect to US Route 9 which connects to the southern terminus of the Garden State Parkway. In the early stages of development, the Authority tried to obtain financing from the Parkway for the approach road, but to no avail. The Parkway welcomed the ferry traffic, but not enough to help pay for the project.

Delaware connections required a new roadway and a large bridge over a canal in Lewes, which is part of the intercoastal waterway. An agreement was reached with Delaware officials under which the approach road and the bridge would be built by the Delaware State Highway Department. The project was eligible for 50 percent federal financing and the Authority paid the remainder of the cost. This roadway was completed about four years after the ferry project began.

This aerial shot shows the location of the then to be constructed Route 9 connection point for the new ferry terminal area in Cape May.

Dredging

At the beginning of the ferry project, it is probable that the single most important activity related to the ferry crossing was dredging - not that it was planned that way.

The engineer's report merely stated, "all channels will be dredged to provide three feet of water below the bottom of the deepest draft vessel at extreme low tide in protected waters and six feet below in open water."

This report, however, did not mention the actual numbers. For instance, the deepest draft vessel required 14 feet of water and a six foot extra depth meant dredging to a level some 20 feet below the water level.

So, in Lewes a normal 6 to 8 foot depth had to be dredged to -20 feet. In Cape May, the situation was similar. In the Cape May Canal, however, the Corps of Engineers was required to maintain a 12-foot channel. Since few vessels at that time required this depth, it was seldom dredged. Despite many political efforts, the Corps refused to dredge the area to the required depth. The Authority was saddled with this job if it wanted to see the ferry service started.

Dredge pipeline propped up over Cape Henlopen Drive in Lewes carries material being dredged from the Lewes Terminal to a disposal site.

Things were even more difficult at Crow Shoal. In this open water area, thousands of yards of material had to be removed from the dredging site. The channel area was dredged to a 500 foot width and a 25 foot depth. The normal water depth was about eight feet. The Crow Shoal dredging proved to be a headache as the area began to immediately refill as soon as the dredging was completed.

Not only was the cost of the dredging unanticipated, but the frequency was a complete surprise. To add to the problems, environmentalists began questioning the effect of the dredging, and it was becoming increasingly more difficult to dispose of the dredged material.

One rather expensive solution to a dredging problem did arise. At the Cape May Terminal, the Authority planned to have a disposal area for the material taken from the canal at a site about a mile south of the terminal. The property had been purchased, the contract awarded and the state permit obtained, when the state, to satisfy some local environmental concerns, decided to withdraw the permit only a few days before the dredging was to start. Then to satisfy local political interests, the Authority was encouraged to purchase a large tract next to the new ferry terminal and use it as a disposal area. This change in dredging plans added another million dollars to the ferry project.

In another instance, the Authority made arrangements to dredge areas at the Lewes Terminal and at the Cape May Terminal and requested the necessary state permits as they had done before. Each state required a separate permit and each state required a study to determine the effects of the dredging on marine life in the area. The Authority was forced to pay $40,000 each to the University of Delaware and to Rutgers University to undertake identical studies. Then the permits were issued and the dredging performed.

Reports containing these study results were delivered to the Authority nearly six years after the dredging was completed! (Incidently, there were no discernible adverse effects on the marine life). It is little wonder that dredging became the most important aspect of the ferry project.

Dredged material from the Cape May Terminal site was dumped in a spoil disposal area just east of the terminal.

This February 1966 photograph of the Cape May Terminal area could be mistaken for the Artic Sea. Ice in the bay has caused ferry service to shut down numerous times.

Ice in the Delaware Bay

Since the beginning of ferry service on July 1, 1964, the most pressing problems during winter months are the ice conditions in the bay.

When the ferry service started, engineers estimated that the service would be interrupted about five days each year, due to inclement weather. The predictions have not occurred. Bad weather has occasionally delayed service, but the delay is usually a matter of hours not days. On the other hand, ice delays which were not foreseen by engineers are more serious and at times, considerably more lengthy.

In 1977 for instance, the ferry service was stopped for 45 days by extreme ice conditions which lasted from January 11, 1977 until February 25, 1977.

During this time period, solid ice surrounded the ferry terminals in Cape May and Lewes. The entire river in early February of that year was 90 percent ice covered. Satellite photos detailing the ice conditions were taken daily.

Earlier in 1970, there was a 12 day ice delay, in 1971 and again in 1979, there was a 10 day shutdown. In 1981, service was delayed for nine days.

When heavy ice forms in the lower Delaware Bay, the ferry service will certainly be curtailed.

CHAPTER 5

BITS AND PIECES

Studies

The 1956 ferry service engineering report described the ferry route, outlined operational conditions and contained construction cost estimates. It did not discuss:
- Terminal building expenses.
- Approach road costs.
- Dredging areas to deposit the dredged material.
- Anticipated traffic usage or revenues from the traffic.
- Probable toll charges.

The report suggested that two vessels would be used, on an 18-hour-per-day schedule, 365 days per year. There was no provision in the schedule for summer and winter traffic demand.

In 1963, more scrutiny was applied. When the Authority met June 11, 1963, it voted to proceed with the financing and establishment of a Cape May-Lewes Ferry system, and also:
- Designated investment bankers to handle the revenue bond for the new ferry project.
- Designated bond counsel for legal problems and conditions relating to the financing.
- Designated traffic engineers for the toll and revenue studies for the ferry.
- Designated consulting engineers for the construction and maintenance and operational features for the ferry.

Within a year, the first Cape May-Lewes ferry would be transporting cars and passengers across the Delaware Bay.

Loran C

All passenger carrying vessels of the type used on the Cape May-Lewes Ferry system are required by the U.S. Coast Guard to have a special navigating device known as "Loran C" equipment.

The equipment, through radio waves sent to receiving stations scattered around the world, is used to advise the ship operators of the position of the vessel. The captain of the vessel not only knows his position at any time but also the time it has taken to reach that position from his point of beginning and the time it will require for him to reach designated points on each trip.

For example, the captain knows within seconds the time he will be adjacent to the outer breakwater in Lewes Harbor. He also knows, regardless of weather or visibility, of his approach time to enter either ferry terminal.

The positions are illustrated for him on a computer recorder constantly changing as the vessel moves through the water. In addition, the route is plotted on maps, and the location of the vessel can be superimposed thereon.

Engineering Report

One must remember that the initiation of the ferry service had all the indications of a real "hurry up" job. One month after the engineers were selected to prepare a report on the "feasibility" of a ferry service, the Authority agreed to purchase the fleet of ferry vessels from Virginia, without a feasibility study, without a revenue study.

The engineering report was not submitted to the Authority until February 24, 1964. Three months before, at the November 1963 meeting of the Authority, commissioners were told:

- The survey work for each terminal was complete.
- The Lewes Terminal approach road survey was complete.
- Bids for the Lewes Breakwater would be opened December 2, 1963.
- Dredging and bulkhead contracts for Lewes and Cape May would be ready December 1, 1963.

Nevertheless, the engineering report submitted to commissioners in February contained the following items:

- The report was based on the acquisition of the ferries from Virginia.

- All of the work could not be completed by July 1, 1964, the scheduled opening date.
- The construction of a stone breakwater at Lewes would add five to ten operating days to the ferry and reduce dredging in the harbor area.
- Toll collection arrangements would be similar to those used on the Chesapeake crossing; passenger cars on a unit basis and trucks by the length of the vehicle.
- The 1965 maintenance and operating cost would be $2.3 million.
- The total cost of construction would be $8.3 million.
- Total project cost including engineering, rights of way and other costs would be $12.65 million.

The newly purchased fleet at dock at the Cape May Terminal in 1965. The ships were (left to right) the SS Delaware, SS New Jersey, SS Cape May and the MV Cape Henlopen.

Ferry Details

After the Authority acquired the four ferry vessels from Virginia, commissioners decided to rename the vessels to reflect their new environment. In a truly bi-state effort to show partnership, the vessels were renamed as follows:

A. SS Pocahontas became SS Delaware
B. SS Princess Anne became SS New Jersey
C. SS Del-Mar-Va became SS Cape May
D. MV Virginia Beach became MV Cape Henlopen

Other details relating to each vessel:

	Length (feet)	Beam (feet)	Draft (feet)	Power	Speed (mph)	Ton Displacement	Veh.	Pass.
A	376	65	10.5	Steam	16	3,195	105	1,200
B	350	59	10.5	Steam	16	2,730	95	1,200
C	350	59	10.5	Steam	16	2,758	95	1,200
D	327	50	9.5	Diesel	14	1,790	75	1,000

The vessels were to be repainted and reconditioned at a cost of $415,000. Of course, beauty is in the eye of the beholder, and, at that time, there seemed to be much more interest in the color scheme for the ferry vessels and the image to be projected on the "smokestacks," than in such routine items as dredging, crew requirements, water depth and other important considerations.

Other Projects

There were at least four additional projects undertaken to prepare for the ferry service which were not considered in the early planning of the ferry system. Perhaps a few words concerning each of these will add to our knowledge of this important transportation service between Delaware and New Jersey.

• Lewes Terminal Jetty

Engineers recommended this jetty to protect the Lewes Terminal area from rough water conditions and also to prevent sand along the shore line from entering the terminal area. The success of this project is obvious; one has only to look at the immense buildup of coastal area adjacent to the jetty at Lewes. The jetty has been, and will continue to be, one of the more important physical additions to the Lewes facility. The project cost was $1 million. The turning of the vessels in the Lewes Terminal area is greatly facilitated by the addition of this jetty.

• The Icebreakers

Years ago, in order to reduce the hazards to shipping in and near the mouth of the Delaware Bay, constant efforts were made to assist mariners. Breakwaters were erected, channel markers were installed and channels were dredged.

The entrance to the bay was particularly hazardous. In stormy weather, the vessels were at the mercy of the prevailing wind, and in winter, ice could be especially troublesome.

One addition to the outer breakwater at Lewes was the installation of the series of stone piles which were placed at intervals of perhaps 50 feet; the intent of the piles was to provide a method of breaking up ice floes as the tide and current moved the ice across the area where the piles were placed. It is doubtful that they were effective.

Shortly after the ferry operation started, the idea of removing a few of the ice breaker piles adjacent to the breakwater jetty was approved. The gap in the icebreaker chain resulted in a slightly reduced distance in the crossing; it also provided a supply of hard-to-get large stones for the next project.

• Cape May Jetty

The existing pair of stone jetties protecting the approach to the canal at Cape May were some 500 feet apart, a relatively tight squeeze when a ferry vessel and a privately owned yacht or other canal users were passing each other in this area.

Accordingly, two projects were tied together. With the approval of the Corps of Engineers and the Coast Guard, the ice breakers were removed and the stones were used to relocate and rebuild the south jetty at Cape May at a distance of 675 feet from the north jetty.

The net result was a shorter route for the ferry crossing and a safer approach to and from the Cape May Terminal area.

• Rip Rap—Lewes

The continuous turning of the ferry vessels as they turned around at Lewes and reversed the engines to back into the ferry slips generated considerable water motion. Adjacent to the ferry terminal on the south side, storage tanks and other property of the Fish Products Company were placed in some danger as the erosion ate away the shoreline land. In order to provide permanent protection, the Authority and the property owner agreed to a procedure where large stones would be placed on the shore to protect the area. The stones, quite visible today, were placed in 1966 and have solved the erosion problem quite satisfactorily to date.

Above: The shore line south of the Lewes Terminal began to erode after construction was completed.
Below: Large stones were placed on the shore to protect the area.

The new jetty (far right) begins to take shape 175 feet east of the existing jetty which was removed to widen the channel at the Cape May Terminal and permit safer passage of ferry vessels.

A Tale of Two Ferry Boats

Captain "A" left Lewes at 1 p.m. on a bright, sunny summer day in late August. At nearly the same time, Captain "B" had departed from Cape May. They would pass each other enroute to the opposite side of the bay. Visibility was excellent, each ferry was almost fully loaded and many passengers were aboard. The bay was busy with normal shipping activity, and many pleasure boats were in sight. It was a nice day for a ferry ride. At about a 3 to 4 mile distance, each ferry was in sight of the other and the radio equipment in each vessel was operating correctly. At about one mile distance, the ferry vessels seemed headed directly towards each other as though one couldn't decide which path to take. Or, as one could say, they were playing "chicken."

At 1,000 yards, the two captains in desperation took emergency action and steered hard right. The two ships bumped each other lightly.

But those aboard were frightened. In one letter sent to the Authority following the incident, a man said he was so scared about his wife's lack of ability to swim, he soiled his trousers!

The Authority and the Coast Guard scheduled hearings for the two captains; each was given appropriate disciplinary action. Each stated he didn't know what course the other was going to take. This event took place more than ten years ago, but it will always be remembered.

Schedules and Tolls

The combination of length of trip time, number of vessels in service, number of vehicles to be transported across the bay and the variance between summer and winter and also daytime and nighttime demand were factors which had to be considered in preparing a ferry operating schedule.

The staff has one idea about operating schedules, the traffic engineer, as he searches for revenue, has another; the user wants frequent crossings.

In 1956, with a two boat operation, the engineering report suggested that the daily schedule start at 6 a.m. and continue until midnight, with no consideration given to summer or winter traffic demand.

When 1963 came, however, the Authority selected a traffic engineer to prepare a report detailing anticipated traffic and revenue at the new ferry crossing. The study was based on extensive field investigations, route reconnaissance, time and distance studies and other factors. The report, submitted to the Authority in early 1964, assumed:

- The service would start July 1, 1964.
- The access roads in Cape May and in Lewes would be completed.
- The proposed vehicle and passenger toll schedules and rates would be adhered to.

In all probability, the traffic engineers were influenced by the availability of the four ferry vessels from the Virginia operation and the 24-hour schedule implemented there. Engineers proposed a two-vessel, 24-hour, year-round operation with a third vessel operating daily in the summer months.

In the same report, suggested tolls were set at $3.25 for passenger vehicles and 75 cents for the driver and other passengers. Trucks were to pay varying fares depending on the length of the vehicle.

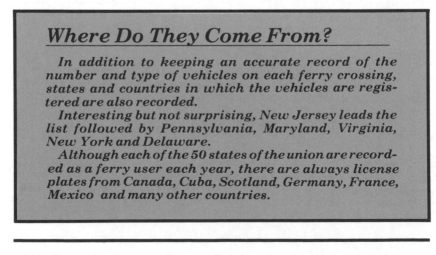

Where Do They Come From?

In addition to keeping an accurate record of the number and type of vehicles on each ferry crossing, states and countries in which the vehicles are registered are also recorded.

Interesting but not surprising, New Jersey leads the list followed by Pennsylvania, Maryland, Virginia, New York and Delaware.

Although each of the 50 states of the union are recorded as a ferry user each year, there are always license plates from Canada, Cuba, Scotland, Germany, France, Mexico and many other countries.

Cars from each of the 50 states and several foreign countries have made the ferry trip across the Delaware Bay.

Traffic and Revenue

With the toll system and the schedule established, the engineers then turned their attention to the all-important bottom line item: How much money could be expected to be collected at the toll booths and how many vehicles and passengers would use the ferry service?

Estimating traffic usage for a ferry crossing project is not an easy assignment. Nevertheless, the Authority wanted an approximate projection of these figures. In analyzing the question, engineers reviewed the motor vehicle use trend in each state and in the region, relating travel time, distance and costs via alternate routes. They also evaluated the economic impact of the ferry on the area, and by using origin and destination studies, assigned traffic volumes to the ferry on a seasonal basis and in turn, on a daily basis.

Estimated revenue was developed from these calculations. Engineers estimated $1.84 million would be collected from an anticipated 280,000 vehicles and 805,000 passengers in 1965.

Unfortunately, the engineer estimates proved to be inflated; 1965 revenue reached only $900,000 from the 170,000 vehicles using the ferry.

The blue and gold Cape May-Lewes Ferry trailblazer.

Ferry Trailblazers

Scattered over a 300 mile distance from New York to Norfolk are about 200 blue and gold trailblazer signs signalling motorists they are enroute to the Cape May-Lewes Ferry. Most major bridges, turnpikes and other prominent points of interest use trailblazer signs to inform motorists of their destination.

Motorists can suggest new sites where trailblazers would be beneficial by writing to the Authority.

Other Income

The traffic engineer report noted that added income could be expected from food and beverage service aboard the ferry vessels and in the terminal areas. The facilities in each terminal area and on each vessel provide needed service to the passengers as well as a viable source of revenue for the ferry system.

What Happens to the Money?

Contrary to the impression many people have, the States of Delaware and New Jersey do not share in the toll revenues collected at the Delaware Memorial Bridge or at the Cape May-Lewes Ferry.

All funds collected plus those earned from investments are retained by the Authority exclusively. They are used for the following purposes:

- *To pay the interest on the revenue bonds which paid for the projects undertaken by the Authority.*
- *To pay for the amortization costs for the bonds on a fixed schedule. All bonds are due to be paid off in 2004.*
- *To pay for operating and maintenance costs for the bridge and ferry.*
- *To pay for other projects the Authority undertakes.*

If the Authority has unspent funds, they are deposited in the Reserve Account and invested by the Trustee.

If the reserves drop below 120 percent of the operating costs, the Authority will raise toll rates or reduce costs to satisfy this condition.

CHAPTER 6

PACKAGING THE PROJECT

Financing

Earlier in this narrative, special attention was given to the creation of the bi-state Delaware River and Bay Authority as the keystone towards solving the financing problems for the initiation of ferry service between the lower end of New Jersey and the southern limit of Delaware.

Each effort in earlier years to encourage the start of this crossing met either with resistance from those who thought that the ferry could not be financially successful or a lack of interest generally in the project.

The passage of the legislation which created the Authority, however, created a different attitude. Now there was a financing method, and a highly successful and profitable one: the Delaware Memorial Bridge. As long as the bridge revenue could be used to pay for ferry activities, the lawyers, bankers, politicians and others could see a rainbow of financial satisfaction.

All of these financial conditions were thought to be satisfied when on April 21, 1964, the Authority voted to approve resolutions which:

- Authorized the issuance of $103 million in revenue bonds.
- Of these, $77 million would be in term bonds at 3¾ percent interest; the remainder in serial bonds at 4 percent.
- Provided for the redemption of the then outstanding bonds from the first Delaware Memorial Bridge.

The official statement relating to the bond sale contained the following:

Outstanding Bonds Redemption	$15.20	
Second Bridge	84.50	
Ferry Project	12.70	
Sinking Fund and Contingency	9.04	
		$121.44 million

Less:

Disbursements to Date	$ 1.44	
Cash on Hand	12.00	
Investment Earnings	5.00	
		$18.44 million

Principal Amount of Bonds $103 million

The money was now available for the ferry projects. Most of them were underway when the bond sale was authorized. The next date to look forward to was the opening date scheduled for July 1, 1964.

Manning a Ferry

The U.S. Coast Guard has regulations specifying conditions all vessels must meet to operate safely. Special rules govern the operations of passenger carrying ferry vessels.

The ferry vessels are inspected regularly by the Coast Guard and each vessel is drydocked every 18 months for more extensive investigation. The regulations also specify the number and type of crew each vessel must maintain.

When the ferry service first began in 1964, 23 crew members manned the 24-hour ferry operation.

In 1970 with the introduction of an 8-hour work day, a crew of 14 was needed on the older steam powered vessels.

The new diesel powered vessels only require nine crew members, far less than the 23 used 20 years ago. The current crew, as required by the Coast Guard, consists of a captain, chief engineer, mate, boatswain, three able bodied seamen and two ordinary seamen.

The licensing arrangements require life jackets for all passengers, lifeboats, and life rafts. Lifeboat drills are scheduled regularly.

While painting and regular maintenance work is accomplished at the Cape May Terminal, drydocking is usually done under contract at shipyards in Norfolk, Virginia, Baltimore, Maryland and Chester, Pennsylvania.

Construction - What, How, Why?

There was much more to initiating a ferry service between Cape May and Lewes than just sailing the ships to the Delaware Bay from Norfolk and starting off. Facilities had to be constructed on both sides of the bay which took considerable time and planning.

The work to be performed was straightforward: Terminals had to be built at Lewes and at Cape May, along with the necessary approach roads, parking lots, buildings, fuel tanks and maintenance buildings. Dredging the terminal facilities and shallow areas in the crossing was another major component in the construction phase of the project.

The engineering report outlined a construction program to meet a July 1, 1964, opening date for the ferry service. Though this

The Lewes Boomerang—not as noticeable from land, but by air, the Lewes Terminal jetty looks just like a large northbound boomerang.

The Boomerang

On the north side of the Lewes Terminal, a boomerang-shaped pile of stones reaches from the shore outwards to form a protective shield for the ferry terminal.

Surprisingly, it was almost an afterthought. When the jetty was suggested, the nearly $1 million estimate made Authority commissioners swallow hard for it had not been included in the original budget.

Nevertheless, the project was approved, primarily because everyone was convinced that the jetty would add some five to ten days of good operating for the ferry by protecting the Lewes Terminal area.

The build-up of sand on the beach adjacent to the jetty proves that it intercepts a strong sand movement. The jetty also provides much better surface water conditions for operating the vessels during storms.

report wasn't available until February 1964, the Authority anticipating the engineers' plan, began construction in late 1963 immediately after acquiring the fleet of ferry vessels from Virginia.

All of the work was done by contractors working for the Authority. In Cape May, one contractor placed the sheet piling and fender piling to outline the ship berths, added transfer bridges to permit vehicles to go aboard the vessels and dredged the area at a cost of $4.1 million.

Above: Site of the Lewes Terminal before construction in March 1964. The pier was part of the Fish Products Factory which was destroyed by fire in the 1960's.
Below: By the end of March 1964, pile driving was underway, and the shore area was cleared for the new Lewes Terminal construction.

Above: Surprisingly, this photo was taken the day the ferry service was dedicated! As you can see, a vessel is tied up at the Lewes dock, while workers furiously continue construction. Below: Though the Ferry had been operating nearly two months, the Lewes pier was just nearing completion in August 1964.

Above: Approach road to the Cape May Terminal was under construction here in this June 1964 photo.
Below: Cars were loading and unloading at the Cape May site while construction of the administration building was just getting started in September 1964. In the background is the fuel tank.

Similar work in Lewes had a price tag of $1.7 million. In the harbor area in Lewes, a breakwater was added to protect the ferry terminal area from waves in high wind and storms.

The approach roadway in Cape May initially cost $450,000, and incorporated the use of an existing township road, Lincoln Boulevard. And in 1980, the Authority completed the dualization of the approach road paralleling Lincoln Boulevard, at a cost of $1.1 million.

The Delaware State Highway Department built the Lewes approach road at a cost of $1.3 million, shared by the Authority and the federal government.

While the roads were being constructed, contractors were building the terminal buildings at Lewes ($90,000) and Cape May ($350,000). In the latter case, a 55,000 barrel (2.3 million gallon) storage tank was erected for the Bunker C fuel storage for the vessels.

One ferry slip was in operation at Cape May when the service opened in June 1964.

Close-up of a pile cluster near the Cape May Terminal. The clusters assist in the maneuvering of the ferry vessels.

By the end of 1964, the Authority had spent or contracted to spend $10.7 million on the ferry projects.

All of the work was not completed by the July 1, 1964 opening date. As a matter of fact, not enough work had been completed by that date to permit the start up of the ferry service in a safe manner. Yet, those interested in the ferry project could see that if the heavy summer resort traffic period passed by, in effect, another year would be lost. So it was decided to start the ferry service —even on a limited basis. To put things into perspective, it is noted:

- There were no terminal buildings at either Cape May or Lewes.
- The berths for the four ferry vessels at Cape May were not finished. Only two vessels could be accommodated.
- Only one transfer bridge was completed in each terminal.
- The ships had never been in either terminal area until the opening date. They had been moored at another dock near Lewes.
- Fuel had to be supplied by truck until the storage tank at Cape May was erected.

Thumbs Up

The dedication of a ferry usually is a local or, at best, a regional attraction. The governor of the state which the ferry serves is invited to attend, and his wife usually christens the ferry by breaking a traditional bottle of champagne.

When the MV Delaware was dedicated, there was more than the usual interest in the event throughout the country. The story was picked up by newspapers across the country.

A special glass is usually used for champagne bottles so it will break rather easily; a nylon web surrounds the glass to prevent it from scattering after the bottle breaks.

However, an enterprising assistant from the naval architect's staff thought the nylon was too fragile and reinforced it with heavy-duty tape.

When Delaware Governor Sherman W. Tribbitt's wife swung the bottle over the steel, it did not break. She swang a second time - and a third time. The Chairman of the Authority assisted her, and on the fourth try the bottle broke, but only after fracturing his thumb.

Yes, the world soon knew that we had christened a ferry.

Ferry Dedication Ceremonies—Invited guests, including dignitaries and politicians from Delaware joined those from New Jersey and boarded the SS Cape May in Lewes to journey to Cape May for the event.

Dedication Ceremonies

Dedication ceremonies for the Cape May-Lewes Ferry were held Tuesday, June 30, 1964 at 11 a.m. at Lewes and at 2 p.m. at Cape May.

The official program contained pictures of the newly acquired ferry vessels, a chronology of construction activities and a list of prominent officials for the speakers platform headed by Governor Elbert N. Carvel of Delaware and Governor Richard J. Hughes of New Jersey. The commissioners and staff of the Authority and political personalities from each state were recognized.

The ceremony ended; the ferry service was ready to begin.

CHAPTER 7

THE EARLY YEARS

The first ferry vessel departed from Lewes at 6:47 a.m. on July 1, 1964, seven minutes later than the scheduled 6:40 a.m. departure. The ferry carried eight vehicles and 15 passengers. The first ferry leaving Cape May carried six passenger cars, a truck, a mobile trailer and 26 passengers.

A slow start, to be sure. But each day showed improvement as more people chose the ferry route. As the ferry crew became more experienced, public interest in the ferry continued to grow. Generally, it was felt that "once the bugs are ironed out, things would be better."

By the end of the first month, 27,250 vehicles and 107,000 passengers had crossed the bay on the ferry, generating nearly $170,000 in revenue. While officials had hoped for greater numbers of passengers, little more could be expected, considering the fact that construction on the terminals had yet to be completed.

The Authority was optimistic. However, more problems were to develop.

Operating problems relating to continuing construction were bad enough, but in late August, just a month after ferry service began, the crew went on strike, shutting down ferry service for 17 days, including the entire Labor Day weekend. The strike generated considerable press interest. Dates selected for the walkout not only interrupted the peak summer traffic period, but also came at the end of the National Democratic Convention which had been held at Atlantic City that year. Politicians who headed south via the newly instituted ferry service were shocked and dismayed to reach the Cape May Terminal area and find the ferries docked, causing them to turn around and head for the Delaware Memorial Bridge, some 90 miles away.

Red Rover, Red Rover, We Did Come Over

Shortly after the ferry began operating, the General Manager of the Delaware Memorial Bridge received a letter from some old friends who rode the ferry in August 1964 and wanted to share their recollections.

One of them suggested the ferry ride to return to Delaware from Stone Harbor, New Jersey. The others said they were making a novena to ask the Lord to forgive the one who suggested the trip.

The author described the approach road in Cape May as "first a filled in swamp, parading under the name of access road, a series of hills and valleys. Picture a washboard like one Mother used, magnified one hundred times."

Finally aboard the ferry, they were hungry. The description said, "You couldn't cut this meat, in fact, a sissy couldn't bend it. The bill was $4.35. This dining room should show a nice profit — you pay for the food and leave it there."

His comments concluded: "Get the guy who first suggested this ferry link, handcuff him, tie an anvil around his neck, blindfold him and let him ride to sea in the pilot house."

The report was captioned with the above title.

Striking employees were acting on the guidance and advice of several different marine labor organizations, each interested in signing up those qualified for their unit; the pilots and mates, the engineers and the deck hands each negotiated separately.

When the crews were brought up from Virginia, the base salary for each person was increased 15 percent over the previous levels, and, in addition, a 10 percent increase was granted when they started working at the new location. The 25 percent increase, however, was scoffed at by the union representatives, who promised much more.

The Authority sought an injunction against the strike, and in a few weeks, not only did the courts compel the picketing to stop, but the strike action folded. During the strike period, construction work at both terminals progressed rapidly while taking advantage of the lull in ferry service requirements. With such a troublesome start, it was only fair to wait for the service to get on the right track before judging its imminent success or failure.

The first full year of ferry operations, not including the last six months of 1964, concluded in December 1965. Let's see how things worked out.

Traffic engineers had projected 200,000 vehicles and 377,000 passengers would ride across the bay in 1965. The actual figures were 161,000 and 542,000.

The income figures only reached $970,000 compared with an estimated $1.8 million.

Operating expenses for that year mounted to $3.1 million, producing an operating deficit of $2.1 million for the first full year of the ferry operation.

What, No Ice?

The opening day ferry festivities on June 30, 1964, started with speeches by dignitaries after which invited guests boarded the SS Cape May for the first trip to Cape May. It was a hot, humid summer day. Aboard the vessel, the guests, who were enjoying the calm, balmy seas, soon thirsted for cool drinks.

Unfortunately, there were no refreshments aboard the vessel and very little ice water. Before the trip back to Lewes from Cape May, Governor Carvel sent orders that the ferry could not depart for Delaware until refreshments and ice were on board.

Needless to say, ice was promptly delivered.

Other Details

The Authority was determined to improve the financial situation of the ferry. Commissioners were confident that since the initial construction problems were over, knowledge of the service would become more widespread, insuring greater vehicle usage and more revenue.

The Authority dove into a public relations campaign to market the ferry. Brochures were printed and distributed and commercials about the ferry began showing up on area television stations. Even airplane tow banners told sunbathers stretched out on the New Jersey and Delaware beaches about the ferry service.

The Authority also cooperated with the Ocean Hiway Association in attempting to lure traffic to and from the southern states and as far away as Canada.

Several operating changes were made in 1966 and 1967 in hopes of improving the service's finances. These included:

- Reducing the toll rates to increase traffic and revenue.
- Approving an agreement to use the ferry vessels as fallout shelters in the event of an emergency.

- Reducing the ferry schedule to help decrease operating costs.
- Deciding to sell the MV Atlantic, the fifth ferry vessel acquired after the others had been obtained from Virginia.

The decisions of reducing the schedule and selling the MV Atlantic raised the ire of both New Jersey Governor Richard J. Hughes and Delaware Governor Charles L. Terry, Jr. In a letter to the Authority in September 1966, the Governors stated:

- They disagreed with the schedule modifications.
- The proposed vessel sale should provide funds for a replacement vessel.
- The Authority should renew its efforts to promote the ferry.

A Long Ferry Ride

Shortly after the Authority had purchased the four ferry vessels from Virginia, it had the opportunity to purchase a fifth vessel, the MV Atlantic, for $200,000. The converted LST would be a sister ship to the MV Cape Henlopen and a back up vessel for the proposed four-vessel operation. When the anticipated traffic pattern failed to develop and the need for a four vessel schedule diminished, the Authority decided to sell the Atlantic to a purchaser from Montevideo, Uruguay. After clearance from the United States State Department, the purchaser came to Authority headquarters December 23, 1966, with a $20,000 down payment in checks, bills and coins. (The typing of contract documents and related clerical activities were hardly joyful pre-holiday events.)

The money was deposited, and in January, a crew was flown up from South America to sail the vessel to its new location. The crew came to Cape May during a snowstorm, a novelty for them. Ultimately, they set sail for Uruguay where at last report, the ferry was operating on the La Plata River between Uruguay and Argentina near Montevideo.

When a commissioner inquired about such a long voyage on the Atlantic Ocean for the ferry, the Authority Director quipped, "It's downhill all the way."

Accordingly, the Authority agreed to satisfy the request of the two Governors and again revised the schedule.

In 1966, for the first time, the ferry service was stopped for three days because of severe ice conditions. This condition had not been seriously considered up to that time as a problem for the ferry system.

A $1.5 million operating deficit was recorded at the end of 1966, an improvement over 1965, but hardly satisfactory.

The First Ferry Accident
— First Time Out of the Slip.

The dedication ceremonies for the ferry took place in Lewes and Cape May on a hot, humid summer day full of sunshine and near 100° temperature. Hundreds of people paid $10 to make the first trip from Lewes to Cape May and return. When the ceremonies at Cape May were concluded, the SS Cape May, laden with passengers (vehicles were not carried on the dedication trip), approached the Lewes Terminal about 4 p.m.

As the ferry turned in the harbor area to reverse engines and move back into the slip berth at Lewes, the captain had to maneuver around dredge lines still being used in the terminal area. In turning, he moved the vessel close to a large oil drum marking the location of a dredge pipeline. All of a sudden, the ferry propeller hooked a steel cable holding the oil drum and wrapped it immediately around the propeller shaft rendering it inoperable.

Laboriously, the captain backed the vessel the remaining few hundred yards into the ferry slip with one engine only. The first ferry crossing on the dedication day had ended in a disaster. Hundreds of New Jersey people were stranded in Delaware.

As pointed out earlier, the facilities on opening day were very limited. Even though the ferry crew knew what had occurred, there was no quick way to remedy the problem. Even worse, no one yet knew if other damage had happened. Immediately, the ferry manager called a shipyard in Norfolk, which flew a diver, along with the necessary tools, to the site. About three hours after the incident had occurred, the diver was in the water cutting away the steel cable. There was no damage to the propeller or the vessel.

The several hundred New Jersey passengers finally boarded the ferry about 9 p.m. for the return ride to Cape May. Surely they will never forget the dedication of the Cape May-Lewes Ferry!

Not unexpectedly, the newspapers had a great story for the next day. Forgotten was the enthusiasm, exuberance and pride in the initiation of the ferry crossing. Now all eyes were riveted on the incomplete facilities and the reminders of the opening day problems.

In 1967, the operating loss was $1.1 million and steadily continued to decrease. Increased revenue at that time resulted from the decision to abandon the reduced vehicle toll rate approved in 1965 and to return to the original toll schedule. Also, only one vessel operated during the winter schedule, producing noticeable savings.

Other events surfaced as the ferry continued service in those early years. Among them:

- A requirement by the two states that sewage no longer be discharged into the bay. This requirement was satisfied.
- A requirement by New Jersey that air pollution equipment be installed on the steam vessels; $150,000 was authorized for this purpose.
- Equipment had to be installed to remove silica in the water at the Cape May Terminal at a cost of $9,700. This chemical adversely affected the cooling system in the ferry engines.
- In March 1968, nearly four years after the ferry service had been started, the Lewes approach road contract was completed.
- Crow Shoal had to be re-dredged, and a contract was awarded in 1968 at a cost of $900,000.

At the end of 1968, the various efforts to reduce the ferry operating costs were succeeding. The ferry payroll, which had reached 225 people in mid 1965, stood at 160. The reductions were made possible by cutting back the schedule and the number of trips made.

These were hard fought decisions. Every time a ferry reduction was proposed, an objection was raised. And yet, one could hardly justify a 24-hour operation when statistics clearly indicated that on many early morning trips, there were no vehicles or passengers aboard.

The 1968 operating deficit, nevertheless, was $1.2 million. There was still a long way to go.

Five Years of Ferry Operations

1969 was a memorable year for the Delaware River and Bay Authority. Among the prominent activities were:

- The completion of work on the Delaware Memorial Bridge and the beginning of the one way traffic pattern on the world's largest twin span.
- The July 9, 1969 accident at the bridge, when the tanker, Regent Liverpool,rammed the fender system at the Delaware tower site, causing $1 million damage.
- The fifth year anniversary of the Cape May-Lewes Ferry.

Lewes approach road under construction, looking toward the bridge over the Rehoboth Canal.

The Lewes Approach Road

The selection of a terminal site for the ferry was not a particularly difficult decision. Although the 1956 engineering report recommended the Roosevelt Inlet site, the new ferry manager and ferry captains opted for the open area adjacent to the Coast Guard Station. The approach road to this site would have to cross property owned by the Mayor of Lewes, so he was consulted.

The Director of the Authority met with the Mayor and the Governor of Delaware to discuss the location of the approach road, one was agreed upon.

At a public hearing required for projects using federal financing, the location was criticized extremely by the Mayor's wife while he, among many others, sat passively in the audience.

The approach road was built at the agreed upon location.

It has since been named "The Theodore C. Freeman Highway" in recognition of a native of Lewes who lost his life while training as an astronaut in 1965.

A panoramic view of the completed Lewes Terminal with parking lots, terminal, loading bridges and toll gate.

Looking Back

The Delaware Coast News of December 30, 1932 contained the following article:

"The Coast Guard has been informed that the seven ships lying off the Delaware coast, beyond the twelve mile limit, are loaded with liquor, wine and cordials, anxious to supply Wilmingtonians and others downstate who wish to toast the New Year with their own brand of whoopee.

"And every night, in the dark of the moon, the speed boats of the rum runners play hide and seek with the still speedier boats of the Coast Guard Bases at Cape May and Lewes. So far, the Coast Guard has been able to head off every effort to bring the contraband ashore."

The TV Show

In 1975, NBC television had a show entitled "Movin' On." It depicted events in the travels of a truck driver and his associates as they went about their interesting assignments.

A staff agent contacted the Authority about using a ferry for a segment of one show. The request was for use of the ferry free of charge. In turn, the publicity may stimulate more interest in the ferry service. Finally, a deal was agreed upon: the ferry would be provided at about half the charter rate — something on the order of $2,000 per day at that time — for a one day period.

Next, the script called for a tractor trailer to be dumped from the ferry into the bay, (in the story, the truck was pushed into the bay just before it exploded from a planted bomb). This request was turned down. Everyone from the Corps of Engineers to environmentalists to marine personnel would have opposed the idea.

The one hour adventure drama, starring Claude Akins and Frank Converse, was televised coast to coast in September. The ferry sequence took about 13 hours to shoot and used about 10 minutes of time in the one hour show. The truck dumping scene was faked.

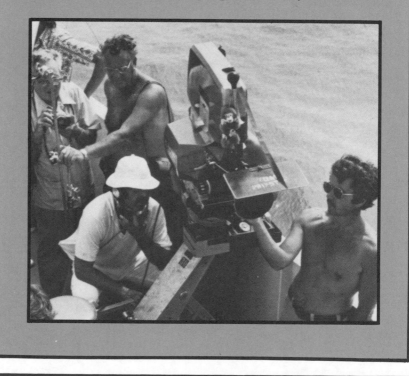

Hot Dogs and Beer

On a typical mid-summer weekend, about 12,000 passengers cross the Delaware Bay on the ferry. In addition to enjoying the balmy breeze off the water and the squeals of children as they feed the seagulls, passengers often spend their time eating and drinking.

In a single day, as many as 800 glasses of beer, 500 hot dogs and 3,000 other beverages are consumed. The food service is operated independently from the ferry by a New Jersey-based food service company. The concessionaire employs as many as 75 people to prepare and serve food during the summer months.

The snack area aboard each ferry serves a variety of food, from breakfasts of bacon and eggs, to burgers, sandwiches and even full-platter hot meals. The challenge is to provide tasty food to huge numbers of passengers quickly.

Souvenirs, newspapers, books and cigarettes, as well as pinball and video games are offered to passengers by the concessionaire, who by contract, must turn over a percentage of the sales to the ferry service.

As soon as the ferry docks at the Cape May Terminal and traffic leaves the vessel, a truck brings supplies aboard. This process gets hectic during the summer months, when turn-around time for the ferries is tight in trying to meet the schedule.

Since the opening date, nearly one million vehicles and some three million passengers had crossed the bay on the ferry. And yet again in 1969, there was a $1.5 million operating deficit.

The Authority's 1969 Annual Report had a banner headline reading "Future of the Ferry" and an article beginning with the statement, "Would abandonment of ferry service matter?" Obviously, the continued financial problems were beginning to hurt.

Since the major source of funds for all Authority projects was the revenue collected from tolls at the bridge, commissioners voted to increase commuter tolls at the bridge from 10 to 20 cents per crossing. This added a relatively small increase in the total picture.

Some of those who objected to the increase blamed the need for it squarely on the ferry and rather loudly denounced it.

CHAPTER 8

THE BIG DECISION

In 1970, the single most important decision in the ferry operation was made, resulting in a substantial reduction in operating costs and noticeably improving the ferry service.

When the ferries served the Chesapeake Bay, the crew adhered to a 24-hour schedule. The entire crew usually worked a seven day on seven day off rotation, which meant the crew lived, ate, and slept on board.

The same type of operation was initiated when the vessels were transferred to the Cape May-Lewes service. However, the new location showed a much different traffic and travel pattern. More seasonal than the Chesapeake Bay traffic, the ferry attracted large numbers in the summer months, but traffic dwindled in the winter. Many trips during the long winter nights had very few passengers; yet the costs of feeding and sleeping the crew continued, along with other operating expenses such as fuel and insurance. It was obvious that the seldom-used night trip needed to be eliminated. But this suggestion ran head on into a political dilemma.

About half of the crew lived in Delaware while the other half lived in New Jersey. A plan was devised proposing that the ferry trips start out from New Jersey each morning. One crew was to work an eight-hour shift, followed by another eight-hour shift which would result in the ferry tied up each night at Cape May to start again in the morning.

This plan would require that the crew live in Cape May which caused the dilemma.

The solution was obtained by a courageous businesslike approach to the problem by Governor Russell W. Peterson of Delaware, who agreed that he would support the plan, though many workers would be moved out of Delaware. The employees were given the option of keeping their jobs and being moved to New Jersey at the Authority's expense or taking severance pay and voluntary leave.

Some chose to stay, others to leave, but the result was that the ferry operating employee list was reduced from 214 in 1964 to 150 in 1969 and to 60 in 1971. The financial problems at the ferry were immediately reversed. At the same time, the basic car rate was increased from the original $3.25 to $4 per crossing.

Out of Fuel

Shortly after the start of ferry operations, following a night trip to Lewes, the Captain called to the Cape May headquarters. "The chief engineer," he said, "advises me that the ferry may be low on fuel."

After a discussion about whether he was sure or not, and why he hadn't filled up at Cape May and other remarks, the operations chief at Cape May decided to risk the return trip. He knew for example, that to be refueled at Lewes would result in a two or three hour delay for the passengers. He advised the captain that if he had problems to call the Coast Guard.

Sure enough, about two-thirds of the way on the trip from Lewes to Cape May, the ferry ran out of fuel and began to drift ... toward Africa.

When the passengers learned of the predicament, they were scared and upset. The call to the Coast Guard provided assistance, but only after a considerable waiting period.

The ferry was then towed to the Cape May Terminal. An investigation by the Authority resulted in the departure of the operation chief who had ordered the return trip, and the exit of the chief engineer because of his negligence.

The problem has never recurred.

Another Big Step

The ferry deficit in 1971 was more than $300,000 less than the 1970 deficit. This reduction in operating costs was even more impressive than usual because it included a dredging expense of nearly a half million dollars at the Cape May Terminal area.

Added to the usual concerns, another incident is worth reporting.

The steam powered ferry vessels used a heavy fuel oil — Bunker C — which had a sulfur content of 2 percent. As environmental interests were more prominently noticed in recent years, the New Jersey air pollution limits reduced the permissible sulfur content to a 1 percent limit. In satisfying this requirement, the fuel prices were doubled.

Most important in 1971, however, was the beginning of the revised operating schedule. The two eight-hour shifts greatly reduced fuel oil consumption and crew requirements.

Cars and walk-on passengers are not the only users of the Cape May-Lewes Ferry. Cyclists also ride up the ramp to make the trip.

Saved Poodle, Sunk Rabbit

In January of 1982 on a late evening trip from Cape May, a Volkswagen Rabbit was loaded among the first vehicles. When the ferry left the slip and turned to go toward Delaware, a heavy truck, parked behind the car, lost its brakes and pushed the Volkswagen off the ferry and into the channel. The owner was in the concession area at the time, but everyone on the ferry quickly knew of the accident.

She had left her poodle in the car among other valuables on her trip from New England to Arizona via Rehoboth Beach where she was to visit her parents.

Fortunately, the car floated in the water until the ferry crew could get a small boat along side and rescue the dog by breaking the rear window.

Then the car sank in the channel. It was retrieved in the morning. The contents were recovered, somewhat the worse for their exposure. Ultimately, the truck owner and the Authority shared in reimbursing the young lady for her losses.

CHAPTER 9

THREE
NEW VESSELS

As operating conditions started to improve, the future of the ferry service was becoming more prominent in the minds of the Authority staff and the commissioners.

The ferry fleet was aging — what should be done?

In the summer of 1970, a report was presented for a long range program for the ferry service. The report recommended that three new ferry vessels be constructed and the older ones disposed of.

The important parts of the report discussed:

- A shallow draft vessel design of not more than 6.5-foot draft compared with 12 feet on the prior vessels.
- The enormous reduction in dredging. With new vessels, there would be no need to dredge Crow Shoal. In addition, the Corps of Engineers would be responsible for keeping the federally required 12 foot channel depth in Cape May Canal.
- New vessels could travel faster, and an increased crossing speed would tighten the schedule.
- Vessels with diesel fuel engines would provide savings over the Bunker C fuel requirements.
- The new vessels would have reduced crew requirements from 13-14 to nine per shift.
- Bow thruster installation on each vessel would provide mobility not available on the older steam powered vessels.
- The new ships would provide the same vehicle occupancy and passenger occupancy as the older vessels.
- The vessels were expected to cost about $2.5 million each.

The decision to go ahead with the purchase of a new ferry fleet was made possible by surplus funds the Authority had saved over the years. The account had grown to about $10 million by the end of 1970.

In March of 1972, Todd Shipyards Corporation of Houston, Texas submitted a bid of nearly $14 million to build three new ferry vessels. After a considerable review, the Authority finally negotiated a contract with Todd to build the three vessels at a cost of $11.7 million.

The contract with Todd was signed in the presence of Governor Russell W. Peterson of Delaware and New Jersey Assemblyman Thomas H. Kean (a future governor of New Jersey) along with the Commissioners of the Authority aboard one of the ferry vessels.

So, a new era in the life of the ferry service was underway. The first of the three ferries was to be delivered in March 1974, the second in June 1974 and the last one in September 1974. As it happened, none of these deadlines were met.

Construction of a Ferry—The next six photographs show progressive stages in the construction of three ferries of the Cape May-Lewes Ferry fleet. This shows midship deck sections in place, ready for fitting.

As 1972 drew to an end, the Authority could look back on an interesting year. Not only was the decision made to proceed with the new ferry construction, but also the revised operating schedule was finally under way. Legislation had been passed permitting the sale of beer on the ferries, the operating deficit continued to decrease, ferry tolls were again increased and U.S. Route 9, a major highway in New Jersey was extended across the Bay via the ferry to Delaware, ultimately connecting with U.S. 13 in Seaford for north-south travel.

The Delaware River and Bay Authority celebrated its 10th anniversary in 1973, which was also the best financial year for the ferry operation since the 1964 opening.

Above: Lowering the starboard main engine of the MV New Jersey into the hull.
Below: Propellers in place on the MV Twin Capes before the rudders are installed.

Above: The hull of the MV Delaware being launched at Todd Shipyards in Houston, Texas. Traditionally, the remaining construction work is completed in the water so that final adjustments can be made there. Below: An interior view of the new ferry.

Completed MV Twin Capes in the Cape May Canal (1977).

Ferry Insurance

A prominent feature in the operation of a ferry system is the budget and one of the most expensive items in that budget is insurance.

Insurance for the ferry vessels is a requirement contained in the agreement under which the bond issue for the project was sold. The insurance protects the Authority and the bondholder against risks incurred during the ferry operation.

Marine insurance coverage is specialized. The Authority has relied on coverage provided by Lloyd's of London in ferry insurance matters. They have proven to be less expensive than coverage available in this country and more cooperative in local coverage conditions.

Nevertheless, it is still expensive. Ferry insurance costs amount to about 10-15% of the annual ferry budget. An example of the rising costs is illustrated below:

Year	Hull Value
1975	4.0 Million
1980	8.0 Million
1985	12.5 Million
1990	14.5 Million

They were built for $4 million each in 1973. The total insurance coverage involves hull and machinery, liability, piers, wharves and docks and the terminal facilities.

One of the old ferries at a dock in Connecticut.

As construction of the new ferry vessels commenced, the Authority staff began searching for a buyer for the old ships.

By coincidence, at the time the new ferry contract was signed, New York officials decided that a proposed bridge connection to the mainland from Long Island should be postponed indefinitely. A move then was underway to initiate a new ferry service connecting the northern end of Long Island with Connecticut or Rhode Island. The Mascony Transport and Ferry Service, Inc. ultimately agreed to purchase the four vessel Cape May-Lewes Ferry fleet from the Authority for $1.9 million.

Ten years before, the Authority had purchased the same four vessels from Virginia for $3.3 million and had spent hundreds of thousands of dollars on repairs. Nevertheless, the sale was a fortunate one for the Authority.

It was not so fortunate for Mascony. The license for the new crossing became embroiled in local politics and never was issued. At last report, the Delaware had been reduced to scrap, the Cape Henlopen had been resold and whereabouts of the Cape May and New Jersey are unknown.

CHAPTER 10

THE TURN AROUND

Governor and Mrs. Sherman W. Tribbitt of Delaware christened the first of the new ferry fleet at the ferry terminal in Lewes, June 10, 1974. The following day, Governor and Mrs. Brendan T. Byrne of New Jersey repeated the event at Cape May. The new vessel, the MV Delaware, began service on the July 4th weekend exactly 10 years after the ferry service had begun. The second new vessel, the MV New Jersey, began service in November of 1974.

1974 also brought with it another decreased budget deficit, down to $615,000 compared to earlier deficits in the millions of dollars.

Inching closer toward a balanced budget, the Authority again raised ferry tolls to $6 per passenger car and $2 for each passenger.

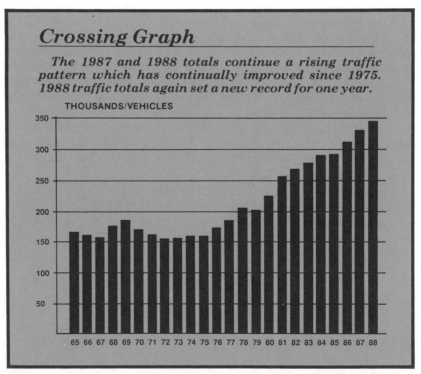

Crossing Graph

The 1987 and 1988 totals continue a rising traffic pattern which has continually improved since 1975. 1988 traffic totals again set a new record for one year.

THOUSANDS/VEHICLES

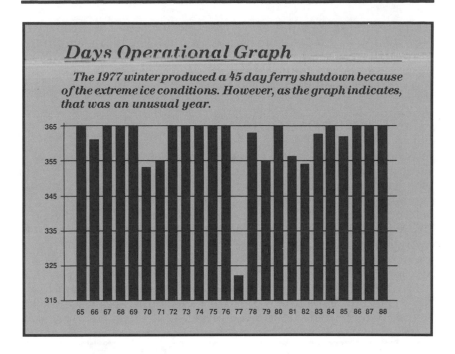

Days Operational Graph

The 1977 winter produced a 45 day ferry shutdown because of the extreme ice conditions. However, as the graph indicates, that was an unusual year.

Black Budget

There was cause for celebrating as 1975 ended. Year-end figures showed that the ferry service operated in the black for the first time, with an $82,000 surplus. The sale of the old fleet had been completed, and the third new ferry vessel was delivered and placed into service. On May 20, 1975, the third ferry, the M V Twin Capes, was christened and shortly afterwards placed into service. The summer of 1975 marked the first summer of the new three-vessel fleet. In August of 1975, the last vessel of the old fleet, the MV Cape Henlopen was sold. The departure on August 17 signaled the end of the 11 year service period by the old ferry fleet carrying passengers and vehicles across the Delaware Bay.

The new ferry fleet operation was accompanied by revised schedules and higher tolls. After the third vessel was placed into service, there seemed to be a turning point in the entire ferry operation.

1976 proved to be a productive year for ferry activities. In that year, revenue again exceeded operating expenses, and vehicle and passenger usage increased.

Among the popular activities was the institution of bay cruises for Cape May County senior citizens. In the spring and fall, thousands of senior citizens took the round trip cruise across the Delaware Bay.

During the same time period, the approach road to the ferry in New Jersey was reconstructed, now a four-lane highway providing a modern, clean approach road for ferry users. The $1.1 million project had been planned during initial ferry construction, but financial problems delayed the construction for 10 years.

A Minor Setback

The ferry staff will long remember the early winter of 1977. Record breaking cold temperatures created severe ice conditions which forced ferry operations to be shut down for 45 days, the most extensive shutdown in the now 20 year history.

Icing started in the upper bay in mid-January. At that time, the Delaware River as far south as the Delaware Memorial Bridge was solid ice except for a single shipping lane. By February 1, all small rivers in Delaware and South Jersey were completely frozen, and ice was present throughout the entire Delaware River.

During this period, the ferry vessels were tied up at Cape May. They could neither enter nor leave the terminal area until the ice cleared, which wasn't until February 25.

Old monument marking the mouth of the Delaware River is retrieved in 1983.

Where Does the Bay Start/Stop?

In 1905, the New Jersey and Delaware legislatures created a six-man commission, three from each state, to settle a long standing dispute between the two states: the dividing line between the Delaware River and the Delaware Bay.

In the 1600's, a deed from King Charles gave Delaware everything in a 12-mile radius of the courthouse in New Castle; this then created the state boundary line at the low water mark on the New Jersey shore. The arrangement left New Jersey crabbers and oystermen at the mercy of Delaware while on the river and within the circle limits, but under federal guidelines while in the bay.

In 1906, the official line was ascertained and marked with monuments. Inscribed on the monument on the New Jersey side is "Mouth of the Delaware River. A straight line drawn from the centre of this monument to the centre of a similar monument, erected at Liston Point, on the Delaware shore, is the dividing line between the Delaware River and Bay..."

In 1983, the Delaware River and Bay Authority after consulting with officials in New Jersey and Delaware engaged a contractor to retrieve the monuments from the river. New platforms have been built on each side of the river based on surveys which accurately designated the exact line on which the monuments are located. The restored markers were placed on the new piers in the later part of 1983.

Delaware shore monument is lifted out of the Delaware River.

Capacity Problems

Ferry traffic and revenues continued to increase. The three vessels were beginning to have problems handling the demands of the summer peak period. Some relief was provided by increasing the number of crossings, but this was only a temporary remedy. Consequently, the Authority began plans for a fourth new ferry vessel.

About the same time, the now famous Atlantic City casino operation was starting. The advent of the casinos significantly increased ferry activity. The fourth vessel would arrive none too soon. Not only would it provide additional backup in the peak summer periods, it would also be available in the event of maintenance problems with another ferry.

CHAPTER 11

MV NEW DEL

The opening of casino gambling in Atlantic City was at least partially responsible for a noticeable increase in ferry usage in 1978.

Vehicle and passenger numbers were the highest in the history of the ferry. In addition, 1978 was the fourth consecutive year toll income exceeded operating costs.

By the end of 1978, the design for the new ferry was nearly completed. It would resemble the other three vessels but would be upgraded to reflect improvements made in the art of shipbuilding in the six years since the other vessels were designed.

The Norfolk Shipbuilding and Drydock Corporation was given the construction contract for the new ferry vessel in August 1979. The new vessel was scheduled to be delivered in early 1981. The contract price was $10.7 million, nearly as much as the three ferry vessels cost in 1972.

The hull structure and the main deck of the MV New Del under construction in Norfolk, Virginia.

The MV New Del poised and ready to be moved from the launchway to the drydock.

The MV New Del ready to go to sea.

Twin Screw vs Double Enders

When the Authority decided to purchase the ferry vessels from Virginia, it automatically accepted a ferry operating procedure which was dictated by the type of vessel to be used.

Many ferry vessels are called "double enders," with propellers on each end of the vessel. In turn, there is no need for the ships to turn around. On the other hand, when the propellers are located on the stern only, such as those in use on the Cape May-Lewes Ferry, the vessel must turn after leaving the slip area in Cape May and before entering the slip in Lewes.

In this operation, the trip from Lewes to Cape May is direct. On the return trip, the vessel is turned after leaving the Cape May Terminal and again reversed to approach Lewes and discharge the vehicles.

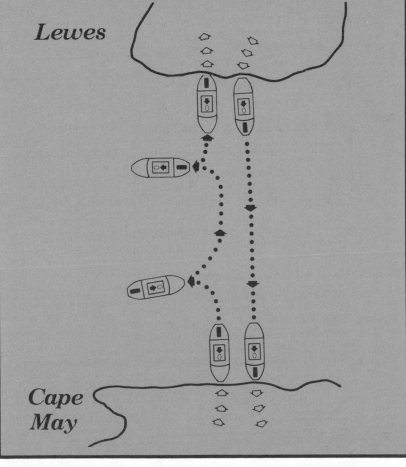

Lewes

Cape May

Governor and Mrs. Pierre S. duPont of Delaware join Authority Commission Vice-Chairman Garrett B. Lyons and Director William J. Miller, Jr. (right) at the christening of the MV New Del.

As in the case of the other three ships, the new one was 320 feet long 68 feet wide with a draft of seven feet. Two 2,000 HP diesel engines would propel the ship at a speed of 15-16 knots across the 17 mile bay area, carrying 100 vehicles and 700 passengers.

In July 1981, Mrs. Elise duPont, wife of Delaware Governor Pierre S. duPont christened the MV New Del and almost immediately the new ferry was put into service.

In 1980 and 1981, vehicular and passenger traffic continued to increase. Paradoxically though, the increased operating costs exceeded the income levels in 1980 by $47,000. However, in 1981 the income, boosted by a toll increase, exceeded operating expenses by $260,000.

The new vessel proved to be a decided asset to the ferry operation. The continued ferry usage — spurred on by the Atlantic City casino — encouraged the Authority to add more crossings to the schedule in 1982 and again in 1983.

In addition, the interest of the senior citizen tours coupled with the now well established Atlantic City bus tours adds even more interest in the ferry.

A story of this type can go on as the years roll by—there never seems to be a shortage of projects. In 1983 and 1984 new sheet piling, new fender piles and new transfer bridges in Cape May and Lewes were erected, at a cost of $3.3 million.

In 1984 construction began on a new terminal building ($1.7 million) in Lewes. The new office and police headquarters was completed early in 1988.

In late 1983, the Authority contracted with Norfolk Shipbuilding and Drydock Corporation for a new ferry vessel—the fifth in the fleet. The 1985 delivery of the MV Cape May assured additional capacity for vehicles and passengers.

When the MV Cape May was delivered, the MV New Del was renamed the MV Cape Henlopen.

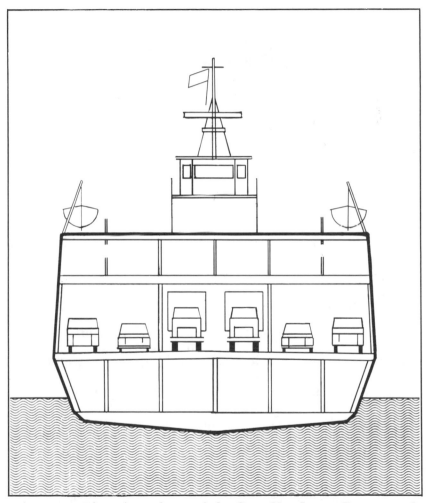

A cross section view of one of the Cape May-Lewes Ferry vessels illustrates the shallow draft conditions. Above the vehicle deck as many as 700 passengers can be accommodated.

CHAPTER 12

NEXT?

In the December 30, 1963 issue of the Atlantic City Press, the headline read, "In Retrospect, A Good Year — Resort Season One of the Best."

The article goes on to say, "The year will probably be remembered most for programs which were initiated during the 12 month period ... to bear fruit for the county in the future ... the most important, the authorization of a ferry line between Cape May City and Lewes, Delaware, slated to be in operation by July 1, 1964."

The article continues, "after 40 years of frustrated effort, the ferry was given a green light on June 11th by an unanimous vote of the 10 member bi-state Delaware River and Bay Authority."

The series of events which have occurred since that time are recorded, in part at least, in this narrative. A chronology would include:

- February 1963   The creation of the bi-state Authority.
- June 1963   The vote to initiate a ferry service.
- August 1963   The decision to purchase the Virginia ferry fleet.
- December 1963   The award of the first ferry service contract.
- June 1964   The dedication ceremonies.
- July 1964   The beginning of the ferry service.
- July 1972   The contract signing for three new ferry vessels.
- June 1974   The dedication of the first ferry, the MV Delaware.
- January 1979   Contract signing for a fourth ferry vessel.
- June 1981   Dedication of the MV New Del.
- September 1983   The decision to build a fifth ferry vessel.
- May 1985   The completion of the fifth ferry vessel.
- June 1988   The completion of new passenger loading buildings, new police facilities and new patron waiting area in Lewes and Cape May.

Feeding the scores of seagulls which follow each ferry across the bay is a favorite pastime of passengers.

Two ferry passengers lean on the rails, watching a beautiful sunset over the Delaware Bay.

Pfc. Richard J. Klochak introduces "Bear" to Police Chief Scott W. Rees, Jr. The golden retriever and his handler are assigned to the Cape May Station.

Authority Police

The continued growth of traffic encouraged the Authority to augment the ferry service by adding police to serve in the terminal areas in Cape May and Lewes and, in addition, to patrol the ferry vessels as they cross the bay.

Police officers were recruited, trained at the appropriate police academies in Delaware or New Jersey and assigned to the Cape May Terminal or the Lewes Terminal beginning in 1986. The officers assist in traffic control for vehicles and pedestrians as they board or disembark the ferry vessels. In addition, traffic on the approach roads in each state is monitored by the Authority police, and also, two police officers are regularly assigned to ride on each ferry as it travels from state to state.

The officers represent about one half of the current 55 person Authority police force. Under the conditions contained in the bi-state compact, "Members of the police force established by the Authority, regardless of their residence, shall have in each State, on the crossings, transportation or terminal facilities and other projects and the approaches thereto, owned, operated or controlled by the Authority... all the powers... conferred by law on peace officers... or usually exercised by such officers in each State."

The unique provision enables the Authority police officers to act in Delaware and New Jersey as police officers aboard the vessels and at the terminals in each State.

You won't go hungry on the ferry. The snack bar serves everything from hot dogs to beer.

Just like a restaurant at sea, these folks eat lunch in the dining area.

Mrs. Jane Sanderson, Administrative Assistant to Mrs. Deborah B. Kean, wife of Governor Thomas H. Kean of New Jersey, dedicated the MV Cape May on May 3, 1985.

Perhaps the most repeated question relating to lower bay crossing activities is, "When will a bridge be built?" or "Will there ever be a bridge here?"

The idea is intriguing, and in all probability there will be at some time in the future, a bridge crossing in this area. Studies which were commissioned by the Authority in 1962 and again in 1970 have focused on a crossing potential in the mid-bay area some 30 to 40 miles above the ferry site. Not only was this idea not financially feasible at that time, but the approach road requirements for such a crossing would delay the project even more. Maybe the year 2000 will bring renewed interest in such a crossing.

A crossing spanning the mouth of the bay is even more difficult to justify. And, considering the many options, the most difficult problem area would be trying to build a bridge along the ferry route. The long distance would be expensive (perhaps a billion dollars in 1983), and a fixed crossing at this location would impose severe restraints on marine traffic in the lower bay area.

Along with these thoughts, let it not be forgotten that the Authority was created not only to provide crossings between the two states of Delaware and New Jersey, but also for the "planning, development, construction and operation of any terminal facilities within both states adjacent to the Delaware River or Bay which is required for the sound economic development of the area."

In 1980, the Authority received a report which addressed some of these conditions. The report entitled, "Present Uses, Potential Developments and Crossing Area Requirements in the Lower Delaware River and Bay Area" was to:

- Analyze the transportation in the area.
- Study the need for additional crossings.
- Examine roles of the agencies in the region.
- Investigate the potentials appropriate for the region.

The report confirmed the feeling that another crossing is some years away. There is, however, the distinct possibility that two or more ferry vessels will be needed and in use before the bridge idea becomes more realistic.

The role of the Authority in port development in the Delaware Bay is addressed in the report. Specifically, the report states, "The Delaware River and Bay Authority is one vehicle available for interstate cooperation in port development." It goes on to relate the potential demand for oil transfer, coal transfer and other multi-purpose usages. Finally, it states that the Authority is the appropriate bi-state agency to undertake such planning.

Numbers and Dollars

- *By the end of 1988, approximately $186.2 million was spent in the construction and operation of the Cape May-Lewes Ferry system.*

- *By the end of 1988, approximately $77.9 million was collected in toll revenue while about $90.8 million was spent in operating expenses.*

- *By the end of 1988, approximately 5.2 million vehicles crossed the Delaware Bay on the ferry along with some 16.6 million passengers.*

- *Three of the present five vessel fleet, the MV Delaware, the MV New Jersey and the MV Twin Capes, were built at Todd Shipyards Corporation in Houston, Texas between 1973 and 1975 at a cost of $12.2 million, approximately $4 million per vessel.*

- *The fourth and fifth vessels, MV Cape Henlopen and MV Cape May were built at Norfolk Shipbuilding and Drydock Corporation in Norfolk, Virginia in 1981 and 1984 for $10.8 million and $14.5 million.*

Each ferry vessel can accommodate approximately 100 vehicles on the six lanes which are on the car deck. The 700 passengers are accommodated on the above deck passenger cabins and added deck areas.

A prudent approach to the overall development of the lower bay area would be served by a long range effort on the part of the Authority (with the concurrence of each governor) to study the feasibility of a deep water port project in the lower Delaware, and perhaps a permanent crossing of the bay with this in mind. The timetable would, of course, depend on the deep draft study results.

There is deep water, necessary for ship traffic, on the Delaware side of the bay. Water depths to 55 - 60 feet extend up the bay to an area known as Big Stone Beach. Heavily laden tankers now bring their cargo of oil to this location; it is then pumped from the tankers into barges and towed up river to the refineries. When the tanker draft reaches 40 feet or less, the tanker can then move up the river to deposit the remainder of the oil.

Now, there is added interest in this area. In 1983, the U.S. Coast Guard issued regulations which permit additional operations in

For the Record

1988 surpassed the 1987 totals which included:

- *The most vehicles carried across the bay in a single year - some 347,000.*
- *The most passengers - some 1,066,000.*
- *The highest income in a single month - $1,806,000.*
- *In 1988 three new facilities were completed to improve the overall operating conditions at the ferry.*
  - *The new passenger loading system at the Cape May and Lewes Terminals separate passenger traffic from vehicle traffic. This, in turn, expedites the movement of the passengers and the vehicles as they boarded and disembarked the ferry vessel. In addition, separate arrangements are included in the system for handicap passengers and vehicle operators.*
  - *The new office and police headquarters building at the Lewes Terminal was completed.*
  - *The new public building and police headquarters at the Cape May Terminal was completed.*

Adding a new ferry—Delaware River and Bay Authority Vice Chairman C.B. McCormick (left), Executive Director W.J. Miller, and Chairman Dr. G.B. Lyons sign contracts authorizing the construction of a fifth ferry vessel in November 1983. The new vessel was built by Norfolk Shipbuilding and Drydock Corporation.

the Delaware Bay area which could result in coal transfer activities. The University of Delaware, in a 1983 report, recommended that the Delaware River and Bay Authority be authorized to monitor all oil and coal transfer activities in the bay.

Since this is the only naturally deep water area on the entire east coast of the country, it certainly should be considered for a port development program at some time in the future. The Authority is the logical agency to proceed with this program.

On July 1, 1984, a ferry service was started which, some say, took 40 years to accomplish.

It is hardly too early today to plan for another crossing and for future port development activities in the lower Bay. The subjects continue to grow in importance. Someday they will be addressed.

Up to Date

Each edition of this book brings changes.

Traffic volumes continue to increase and new records are established only to be surpassed again and again.

When the fifth vessel was placed into service in 1985, it looked as though traffic volumes were manageable. By 1988, it became apparent that conditions had to be reviewed once more.

At this time provisions are being made to provide additional car deck space on each ferry. Additional decks are to be added to each vessel to increase the capacity by 40 vehicles. At the same time additional covered passenger seating areas are also under consideration.

After the double decking is completed, and after the passenger seating expansion conditions are cared for, the next logical consideration will be the addition of a new ferry vessel complete with the design elements that have been added to the present ferry fleet.

Or, perhaps somewhat with a touch of regret, maybe we'll have to more seriously consider a bridge or tunnel to handle the constantly increasing traffic volumes crossing the Delaware Bay.

Indeed, where do we go from here?

The new Lewes Administration Building and Maintenance Garage was completed in 1988 (above). The new 21,000 square foot building at the Cape May Terminal was completed in 1988 (below).

Appendix A - Persons and Patrons

How To Be A Ferry Captain

William R. "Billy Ray" Phillips, now the assistant port captain was, prior to his promotion, the senior captain of the Cape May-Lewes Ferry. Capt. Phillips graduated high school and went to work for the Virginia Ferry Corporation at age 16, sailing as Ordinary Seaman on the ferries crossing the mouth of the Chesapeake Bay. Phillips also sailed on the Ferry Corp. tanker, and received his Able Bodied Seaman certification from the U.S. Coast Guard when he was 19. Phillips sailed as wheelsman and as boatswain during the next two years, earning his First Class Pilot's license at age 21. At age 25, he received his captain's license and began sailing as captain of the Virginia ferries at age 26.

In 1964, the Virginia ferry corporation was replaced by the Chesapeake Bay Bridge Tunnel. When the ferries were sold to the Delaware River and Bay Authority in 1964, Phillips was hired as a senior captain for the Cape May-Lewes Ferry system.

Coast Guard Requirements for Becoming a Ferry Captain

To attain captain — minimum of 4 years working 7 days a week assuming advancement immediate to next position.

1. Beginning as ordinary seaman — need to be hired by company and placed aboard vessel in unskilled status, Coast Guard will document at request of company.
2. Ordinary seamen need a minimum of 365 days of underway sea time to become an able bodied seaman (3 years of days to go to highest Ocean rating).
3. Able bodied seamen need a minimum of 18 months sea time to attain pilot classification.
   (a) At least 2 years combined ordinary seaman & able bodied seaman to become a mate.
   (b) At least 3 years combined ordinary seaman & able bodied seaman to become a pilot.
   A graduate of the maritime academies has all qualifications through mate and needs only necessary trips (currently 24) to qualify for pilot.
4. Pilots must meet either (a) or (b) qualifications to move on to rank of captain:
   (a) 1 year (365 days) sea service as pilot or
   (b) 2 years (730 days) sea service as licensed boatswain or licensed wheelsman while holding pilot's license.

Appendix A - Persons and Patrons

How To Be A Ferry Chief Engineer

George Menge is senior chief engineer of the Cape May-Lewes Ferry. After graduating from high school, he worked in a machine shop until enlisting in the U.S. Navy in July, 1944, where he served four years aboard patrol craft. Menge then transferred to the U.S. Coast Guard, earning his chief petty officer rating in 1949. While in the Coast Guard, Menge served as engineer aboard weather patrol ships in the Atlantic and Pacific. He also served aboard buoy tenders and other Coast Guard cutters, earning his Warrant Officer rating in 1958.

In 1964, he retired from the Coast Guard and worked as port engineer for McAllister Brothers in the port of Hampton Roads, Va. until joining the Cape May-Lewes Ferry in May 1978. Menge has sailed ever since as chief engineer of the Cape May-Lewes Ferry.

Coast Guard Requirements for Becoming a Ferry Chief Engineer

Beginning as wiper (entry rating compares to ordinary seaman in deck dept.).

1. Coast Guard issues document at request of company. Company hires man and assigns to vessel.
2. (a) Wipers need at least 6 months sea service to become an *oiler* or qualified member, engine dept., or,
   (b) graduation from a school ship or,
   (c) satisfactory completion of Coast Guard approved course and service aboard a training vessel.
3. To become a 3rd assistant engineer
   (a) 30 months as QMED, 18 of which must be oiler, fireman or watertender
   (b) graduation from maritime academy
   (c) several combinations of training plus sea time
4. To become a 2nd assistant engineer
   (a) 1 year service as 3rd assistant
   (b) 2 years as junior 3rd assistant
   (c) 5 years total engine time, 30 months of which must be oiler, fireman, or watertender.
5. To become a 1st assistant engineer
   (a) 1 year service as 2nd assistant
   (b) 2 years service as 3rd assistant
6. To become a chief engineer
   (a) 1 year service as 1st assistant
   (b) 2 years service as 2nd assistant

Appendix A - Persons and Patrons

Delaware and New Jersey Joint Conferees

In 1958 the following individuals constituted the Bi-state Conferees Committee who recommended the creation of the Delaware River and Bay Authority as it exists today.

DELAWARE CONFEREES

Hon. J. Caleb Boggs, Governor
Garrett E. Lyons, Director, Interstate Highway Division, Chairman
Senator-elect Reynolds du Pont
State Representative Joseph B. Walls, Lewes
Clair J. Killoran, Wilmington Attorney
James L. Latchum, Attorney for Division and Secretary of
    Delaware Conferees

NEW JERSEY CONFEREES

Hon. Robert B. Meyner, Governor
Senator John A. Waddington, Salem Co., Chairman
Senator Charles W. Sandman, Cape May
Assemblyman John W. Davis, Salem
State Highway Commissioner Dwight R.G. Palmer
Vincent P. Biunno, Personal Counsel to Governor and Secretary
    of New Jersey Conferees

*   *   *   *   *

Governors of the States of Delaware and New Jersey during the period of time covering the planning, construction and operation of the twin span Delaware Memorial Bridge and Cape-May Lewes Ferry.

DELAWARE

Walter W. Bacon	1941-1949
Elbert N. Carvel	1949-1953
J. Caleb Boggs	1953-1960
David P. Buckson	1960-1961
Elbert N. Carvel	1961-1965
Charles L. Terry, Jr.	1965-1969
Russell W. Peterson	1969-1973
Sherman W. Tribbitt	1973-1977
Pierre S. duPont, IV	1977-1985
Michael N. Castle	1985-

NEW JERSEY

Walter E. Edge	1944-1947
Alfred E. Driscoll	1947-1954
Robert B. Meyner	1954-1962
Richard J. Hughes	1962-1970
William T. Cahill	1970-1974
Brendan T. Byrne	1974-1982
Thomas H. Kean	1982-

Appendix A - Persons and Patrons

Authority Commissioners

DELAWARE	NEW JERSEY

ORIGINAL COMMISSIONERS IN 1963

DELAWARE	NEW JERSEY
J. H. Tyler McConnell	Theodore C. Bright
William R. Murphy	Joseph L. Bowe
James T. Ferri	Bayard L. England
James G. Smith	Clarence B. McCormick
Howard S. Abbott	Thomas J. Gallagher

INTERIM COMMISSIONERS

DELAWARE	NEW JERSEY
Alexis I. duP. Bayard	James L. Smith
Benjamin P. Shaw, II	Frank LoBiondo
Alfred F. Smith	LeRoy H. May, Jr.
Walton H. Simpson	John Vinci
Louis E. Edgell	Joseph J. Fabi
Ernest E. Killen	
Francis A. DiMondi	

COMMISSIONERS THROUGH 1988

DELAWARE	NEW JERSEY
Dr. Garrett B. Lyons	William A. Gemmel
James Julian	Walter F.W. Maack
Remsen C. Barnard, III	Angelo J. Falciani
Alfred Leo Donnelly	Jack Sparks
(Vacancy as of 12/88)	(Vacancy as of 12/88)

Appendix A - Persons and Patrons

The Ferry Work Force

Many people are involved in the operation of the Cape May-Lewes Ferry. They include:

6 — The General Manager and his staff including Port Captain, Port Engineer, and secretary.

25 — The ships' officers including Captains, Pilots, Mates, Chief Engineers, and Assistant Engineers.

27 — The ships' crew including Bosuns, Abled Bodied Seamen, Oilers, and Ordinary Seamen.

8 — The machine shop and engine maintenance crew, electrical/electronics and carpentry shop workers.

23 — The Terminal Managers and their staff including Dock Attendants, Storekeepers, Maintenance Workers, and Watchmen.

7 — The Office Manager and his staff of Ticket Sellers, clerical, secretarial, and accounting personnel.

96 — Total

The 1989 operating budget of $9.04 million includes $5.5 million in salary and employee benefits, $0.9 million in insurance premium costs and the remainder for material, services and shipyard costs.

* * * * *

The following people served as General Manager for the Cape May-Lewes Ferry since service was initiated on July 1, 1964.

☐ **Nolan C. Chandler** (1963 - 1968)
☐ **Theodore C. Bright** (1968 - 1982)
☐ **David S. Chapman** (1982 -   )

Appendix B - Vessel Particulars

NAMES:
MV DELAWARE
MV NEW JERSEY
MV TWIN CAPES
MV CAPE HENLOPEN
MV CAPE MAY

Crossing Distance — 17 miles

Crossing Time — 1 hour, 10 minutes

Length: 320'0", Breadth: 68'0"
Depth: 17'0" Draft: 7'0" (Max.)
Displacement: 2100 Tons +/-
Capacity: 800 Passengers,
　　　　　100 Cars
Main Engines: 2 Diesel, 4000 HP
Generators: 2-300 KW, 1-150 KW
Bow Thruster: 5000 lbs. Thrust

Classification: USCG & ΛBS
Speed: 15-16 Knots
Double End Loading
Single End Propulsion
Snack Bar
Hull Design CE-2096
Cost: $11,720,000 (3)
　　　　$10,754,920 (1)
　　　　$14,500,000 (1)

Naval Architect
Coast Engineering Company (3)
Norfolk, Virginia

J. J. Henry Company, Inc.
Moorestown, New Jersey (2)

Shipyard
Todd Shipyard Corporation (3)
Houston, Texas

Norfolk Shipbuilding and Drydock
Corporation
Norfolk, Virginia (2)

**Exterior Seating for
460 Passengers**

**Interior Seating for
340 Passengers**